P9-CAN-980

COURSE MANUAL
for

Becoming a
Master Student

TENTH EDITION

by

DAVE ELLIS

*Tools, techniques, hints, ideas, illustrations, examples,
methods, procedures, processes, skills, resources, and
suggestions for designing and delivering a college or
university college survival course*

Houghton Mifflin Company

BOSTON   NEW YORK

Sponsoring Editor: Patricia Coryell
Development Editor: Janet Edmonds
Associate Editor: Shani B. Fisher
Editorial Assistant: Andrew M. Sylvester
Senior Project Editor: Rachel D'Angelo Wimberly
Senior Production/Design Coordinator: Sarah Ambrose
Manufacturing Supervisor: Florence Cadran
Marketing Manager: Barbara LeBuhn

College Survival
A Program of Houghton Mifflin Company
2075 Foxfield Drive, Suite 100
St. Charles, IL, 60174

© Copyright 2003 by Houghton Mifflin Company. All rights reserved.

If *Becoming a Master Student* is the required text for your course, you have permission to copy any pages in the *Course Manual for Becoming a Master Student* for use by students in your college survival course. If *Becoming a Master Student* is not a required text for your course or if you would like to use this material in a setting other than your course, contact Houghton Mifflin for permission to copy any pages from the *Course Manual for Becoming a Master Student*. Copies may not be sold, and further distribution is expressly prohibited. Except as authorized above, prior written permission must be obtained from Houghton Mifflin Company to reproduce or transmit this work or portions thereof in any other form or by any other electronic or mechanical means, including any information retrieval system, unless expressly permitted by federal copyright law. Address inquiries to College Permissions, Houghton Mifflin Company, 222 Berkeley Street, Boston, MA 02116-3764.

Printed in the USA.

ISBN: 0-618-23278-8

3 4 5 6 7 8 9 – VG - 07 06 05 04 03

As part of Houghton Mifflin's ongoing commitment to the environment, this text has been printed on recycled paper.

TABLE OF CONTENTS

Copyright © Houghton Mifflin Company. All rights reserved.

Copyright © Houghton Mifflin Company. All rights reserved.

Copyright © Houghton Mifflin Company. All rights reserved.

Copyright © Houghton Mifflin Company. All rights reserved.

Copyright © Houghton Mifflin Company. All rights reserved.

Introduction

Welcome! The *Course Manual for Becoming a Master Student* is designed to assist you in planning the curriculum of your college survival course.

Most instructors' preparation will include the following:

- Writing the course purpose statement
- Establishing course objectives
- Determining instructional choices
- Integrating some technology in the course
- Assessing assignments and exercises
- Identifying evaluation criteria
- Creating and maintaining a supportive classroom atmosphere for college and university students in their first term of higher education as they start on their journey to success

Newcomers to this discipline might consider this manual as an encyclopedia of topics related to teaching college success courses for first-year and returning students. You are not expected to study this manual and implement everything in it any more than we teachers would expect new students to study and implement everything in their college survival course text.

Many of the articles in this Course Manual originally appeared in the *Student Success* newsletter published by College Survival.

   Copyright © Houghton Mifflin Company. All rights reserved.

PART I:
ESSENTIALS FOR PLANNING AND INSTRUCTION

Overview

College Survival, Freshman Seminar, University 101, and the First-Year Experience are among the various names for the most researched and results-oriented course in higher education. This course is designed for learners in their first term or year at a university or college. According to Aubrey Forrest's report for the National Center for Advancement of Educational Practices entitled *Increasing Student Competence and Persistence*:

Probably the single most important move an institution can make to increase student persistence to graduation is to ensure that students receive the guidance they need at the beginning of the journey through college to graduation. At its best, this guidance system should include the following feature: New student orientation should continue as a formal course during their first term on campus.

The purpose of a college survival course is to assist students in navigating the terrain of higher education, to improve their academic performance, to help them determine their strengths and goals, and to encourage them to implement strategies to enhance their personal, academic, and career success.

The content of a college survival course will be influenced by the institutional mission statement, the teacher designing the course, the outcomes expected by the administration, and the profile of the students in the course.

The content of a college survival course might include the following:

- The history of higher education
- Academic proficiency skills
- Self-assessment and inventory
- Critical thinking and writing
- Diversity and international relations
- Listening and speaking skills
- Modes of inquiry
- Oral presentation skills
- Service learning
- Computer competency
- Collaborative learning activities
- Effective use of learning resources and tutors
- Library and scholarship skills
- Campus and community support services
- Research skills, documentation, and academic writing
- Career awareness and portfolio and résumé writing
- Civility in the classroom
- Academic integrity

Competency objectives for a college survival course might include the following:

- To assess and inventory current strengths and areas for growth
- To increase awareness of beliefs, choices, and behaviors

Copyright © Houghton Mifflin Company. All rights reserved.

- To provide use of, knowledge of, and access to campus support staff and programs
- To explore and enhance transferable academic, personal, and career skills

Expectations of student classroom behavior might include exhibiting the following qualities of exceptional employees:

- Self-knowledge and insight
- Preparedness and punctuality
- Involvement and initiative
- Attentive listening skills
- Critical reflection and writing skills
- Creative problem-solving skills
- Respect for the opinions and values of others
- Curiosity and a desire for lifelong learning
- Positive contributions to the climate of the workplace
- Thorough, timely, and thoughtful completion of tasks
- Active participation
- Application of strategies in other areas of study and life

Elements of assessment in a college survival course might include the following:

- Reading assignments
- Written exercises, Journal Entries, and classroom activities
- Individual and small group presentations
- Quizzes
- Conversation and discussion
- Projects
- Final examination
- Evaluation

An effective course framework might be described as follows:

- Credit-bearing
- Built into the curriculum as a core requirement
- Presented over the first term
- Involving 30 or more contact hours
- Taught by the best instructors
- Well scheduled
- Clearly valuable to students and staff

Outcomes of a college survival course might include the following:

- Enhanced student performance
- Increased grade point average (GPA)
- Greater number of courses attempted and completed
- Persistence to graduation
- Enhanced faculty satisfaction
- Partnership in the learning environment

Copyright © Houghton Mifflin Company. All rights reserved.

Starting Points

Congratulations!
You are teaching a college survival course!

Consider this book the "owner's manual" for your college survival course. This manual is designed to streamline your efforts and to give you the best suggestions collected from more than 10,000 educators and the consultants of College Survival, who have more than 18 years of experience implementing premier college survival courses.

You might not choose to explore every section. You might start with the topics about which you require the most guidance or anticipate struggle. You might feel very confident and still choose to enhance or revitalize your areas of expertise.

This is a guide for designing your course and exploring major subjects in all college survival courses. Your HMClassPrep CD-ROM offers you chapter-by-chapter resources. Your planning will result in the creation of a course that will reflect the uniqueness of your teaching style, the personality of your students, and the culture of your campus. Consider this manual as a springboard to many possibilities. Adopt and modify these ideas for your course purpose and structure, and for the outcomes you plan to achieve.

If you have limited time for planning, please do three things:

1. Do the first 15-minute exercise in *Becoming a Master Student*, the textbook reconnaissance exercise. Touch every page of the text. This will give you an overview and will spark your imagination about what to highlight for students.

2. Apply the sample principles of this exercise to the *Course Manual for Becoming a Master Student* to familiarize yourself with the topics.

3. Believe us when we tell you about the partnership available to you as a member of the network of professionals using *Becoming a Master Student*. Just as a teacher will provide information and support to students and will help them choose effective personal and professional strategies, the consultants of College Survival will provide you with information and support for the creative process of designing a course for your students.

Instructional Resources

The following support services and materials are available to you through College Survival. All are free of charge.

HMClassPrep CD-ROM

With chapter-by-chapter resources, lecture ideas, and exercises, the goal of HMClassPrep is to provide you with instructional resources that you can use in electronic form. Each resource is provided in the file format we think will be most useful to you: Word files for documents you might want to edit, video files for presentation, and PDF files for handouts. Most resources can be customized so they match exactly the way you teach your class.

You can access the files on HMClassPrep directly through the HMClassPrep interface. This interface organizes resources for you by chapter or by asset type. Using the HMClassPrep interface, you can open files in their appropriate applications, use them as they are, or modify them and save them to your hard drive.

For more on the HMClassPrep CD-ROM and its contents see page 50 of this manual.

Copyright © Houghton Mifflin Company. All rights reserved.

Educational Consultation and Curriculum Design

You are cordially invited to call College Survival consultants as you plan your college survival course. We are accessible by telephone (at the toll-free number 800-528-8323), via the Web (**http://collegesurvival. college.hmco.com/instructors**), and by fax (800-210-0212). Drawing on our conversations with literally thousands of educators, we will provide you with a sampling of their creative ideas as well as strategies derived from our own teaching careers.

We will provide support as you find new ways to present material, explore exercises to involve students in their learning, expand the credits or sections of your course, and consider innovative ways to present course content and concepts. We will also assist you in discovering strategies to enhance the persistence and performance of your students.

The College Survival Course Workshops and Conferences

These highly interactive workshops provide an exceptional training opportunity for teachers, coordinators, and administrators who are responsible for the design and delivery of extended orientation, study skills, and other college survival courses. Scheduled several times each year, these workshops can help do the following:

- Demonstrate and model the components of an effective college survival course
- Help prepare new instructors for teaching college survival courses
- Offer experienced teachers ideas for course rejuvenation
- Give participants an opportunity for both personal and professional refreshment and growth

Each year tuition is waived for two educators from each school at which *Becoming a Master Student* is a required text. For a list of scheduled events and hotels, speak to a College Survival consultant or visit our web site.

On-Campus Workshops and Trainings

At the invitation of a university, college, or community college, College Survival will arrange a one-day event for college survival course instructors, professors, counselors, and/or administrators. These events present pedagogical strategies that can be effectively applied to all disciplines. The College Survival facilitator, working in collaboration with the campus college survival course coordinator, creates the agenda. The event is tailored to meet the needs of the specific staff, institution, and students being served.

Frequently requested topics include the following:

- Course design
- Objectives and evaluation criteria
- Collaborative learning
- Diversity in learning and teaching styles
- Promoting student self-responsibility
- Creative and effective teaching strategies

For additional information about fees, to schedule an event, or to obtain information on hosting an event for other colleges and universities in your area, call your consultant at 800-528-8323.

Newsletter

The newsletter *Student Success* is mailed free of charge to all teachers using *Becoming a Master Student* as the required text for their courses. The newsletter provides a common forum for instructors to share their experiences and effective teaching ideas. Perhaps the most valuable teaching resource is other teachers. You can take advantage of this resource by subscribing and contributing your thoughts and ideas to the newsletter. You may subscribe to the newsletter and retrieve previous lead articles at our web site, **http://collegesurvival.college.hmco.com/instructors**.

Videotapes

Two free videotapes are available to instructors using *Becoming a Master Student*. One, for use as a first day of class "guest speaker," includes a critical reflection exercise and is titled *What Do You Want?* This course

Copyright © Houghton Mifflin Company. All rights reserved.

introduction videotape has a running time of seven minutes. The second tape prepares instructors to administer the Learning Style Inventory (LSI). This videotape has a running time of 23 minutes. You may order these videotapes by calling Houghton Mifflin Faculty Services at 800-733-1717.

PowerPoint Slides

For each chapter of *Becoming a Master Student*, PowerPoint slides may be downloaded from the web site http://collegesurvival.college.hmco.com/instructors. The PowerPoint slides are also available on your HMClassPrep CD-ROM.

Scholarship Essay Contest

Each year, Houghton Mifflin Company sponsors a scholarship essay contest for students enrolled in a college survival course at an institution of post-secondary education in the United States or Canada. We invite you to nominate one student from your college to be eligible for winning the scholarship.

Host a schoolwide competition for students enrolled in college survival or study skills courses. In your campus contest, have each of your students write an essay on the topic "What is a Master Student?" The essay should not exceed 750 words. We suggest integrating the contest into your fall syllabus as a writing assignment. Consider including it as part of your students' work on Chapter One of *Becoming a Master Student*. You will notice that the Master Student Profile for Chapter One is a previous winner of Houghton Mifflin's scholarship essay contest.

You might also find ways to make the contest even more interesting for your students. For instance, one school is allowing students to be the final judges. The instructors (or students, as the case might be!) at each school decide on one winner for your institution. Send the winning essay and completed entry form to College Survival at Houghton Mifflin. Each school may submit only one entry. Check our web site for an official entry form, the entry due date, and the scholarship prize. Encourage your students to read essays of previous winners on our web site as well.

3x5 Cards

Three-by-five cards facilitate classroom participation, and are provided at no charge to teachers who purchase *Becoming a Master Student*. The text and the HMClassPrep CD-ROM suggest a variety of uses for 3x5 cards. Instructors and students often report becoming obsessed with them. Many have divulged their secret passion for 3x5 cards. They find them lurking in closets, hiding under their beds, stuck on their mirrors, pinned to bulletin boards, tucked into pockets, slipped into their notes, marking their places in books, resting next to their telephones, even replacing their address and recipe books. Some instructors ask students to carry 3x5 cards with them for a few days and jot down how they use their time. By doing so, students can monitor what they are doing and the amount of time they spend doing it.

Another way to use 3x5 cards is for attendance. Have students write their names and a question on a 3x5 card. Then have students bring their cards to class each day to hand in as their admission tickets to class.

Two-Part Exercise Sheets

Two-part exercise sheets (up to five per book ordered) provide a way to encourage students to participate in class. The final step in any classroom exercise can be for students to write Journal Entries on two-part sheets. If you collect the original, letting students keep a copy for their own use, you can read some of the student discoveries and insights anonymously to the rest of the class. Students are interested in what their peers think. Collecting two-part sheets can also be a convenient way to take attendance.

Three-Part Quiz Sheets

To take a more active role in learning, students can participate in grading their own quizzes by using three-part quiz sheets (up to 10 per book ordered). Here's how the process works: Put the quiz questions on a transparency, blackboard, or separate sheet of paper. Ask students to write their answers on the three-part sheet. After students complete the quiz, have them turn in the original white copy. Now ask

Copyright © Houghton Mifflin Company. All rights reserved.

students to look up the answers and to correct and grade their own work. (On the test form, you can indicate the number of the text page where each answer can be found and the date of the lecture so students can refer to their notes.) They then turn in one of the corrected copies and keep the other one for their own use. Students get immediate feedback, and you save time by not having to grade and return individual quizzes.

Course Philosophy

The underlying philosophy of this course is based on the following three assumptions:
1. There are no secrets.
2. There are no victims.
3. There are no solos.

There Are No Secrets

It is usually a mistake to assume that students come to school prepared. As they begin college, they face major changes in their environments and lifestyles. Assuming that they know how to study and how to be effective students is often inaccurate. The fact that students have been in school for years is no guarantee that they have mastered the process of learning.

Most students enroll in college with both the ability and the motivation to succeed. During exit interviews many educators discover that what students lacked was a clear understanding of specific strategies to get what they wanted from school. Most dropout statistics can be lowered when students become aware of learning strategies, experiment with them, find those that work, and turn them into habits that they adopt as part of their daily routines. *Becoming a Master Student* and the course outlined in this manual present clear, positive, appealing images of behaviors that lead to success. As students begin to experiment with and adopt these behaviors, they are on their way to achieving their goals.

There Are No Victims

Blaming other people or circumstances does not empower us to get what we want. Even blaming ourselves gets in the way of success. Blaming cheats us of the experience of taking full responsibility for our lives. Taking responsibility opens the door to making choices that allow us to be in control. The Power Process "I create it all" in the text presents this idea.

There Are No Solos

Human beings are social creatures. Other people play a powerful role in the development of our own values, belief systems, and behaviors. A supportive environment is a critical element of college survival. This course provides an opportunity for students to connect with others and form mutually beneficial relationships. Students can also become aware of the many resources and programs that can promote their success.

Values-Based Education: The Author's Themes

Becoming a Master Student is unique because it is based on a particular value system that is incorporated in all of the study skills throughout the book. This system includes the following five values:
1. Focused attention
2. Personal responsibility
3. Integrity
4. Risk taking
5. Contribution

These values are discussed in a general way in several of the Power Processes presented throughout *Becoming a Master Student* and are the foundation of each of the study skills, life skills, and activities pre-

Copyright © Houghton Mifflin Company. All rights reserved.

sented in the text. For example, when presenting the study skill of note taking, the text is really introducing the concepts of focusing attention, contributing to fellow students by sharing notes, and taking risks by using notes as an opportunity to ask questions of teachers. Also, when talking about time management, the text frequently presents the ideas of focusing attention, being responsible for one's use of time, and practicing integrity.

These values show up even more obviously in the life skills that the text describes as communication, leadership, stress management, and so on. Throughout the course, the instructor can build on these values and reinforce the fundamental concepts of the text by referring back to the Power Processes or by posting the five values previously mentioned and asking students to find examples used throughout the book or presented in class lectures or by guest speakers.

Writing Your Course Purpose

Planning Your Course

Students at each school and the purpose and focus of the course at each institution will be different. *Becoming a Master Student* was designed to give students a variety of topics and ideas. This manual was created to assist you in selecting material most appropriate for your students and course purpose and in fulfilling your institutional mission statement of how your graduates will be unique.

The first question to ask yourself when planning is: Who will take the course? Many colleges across the country require that their new students participate in a college survival course. They feel that this course will be an educational foundation for students in their day-to-day college courses and as they link their knowledge to their future careers. The skills undergraduates use to be effective students (time management, critical thinking, writing, communication skills, and so on) are the same skills that will assist them in becoming effective employees. Significant research over the past 25 years acknowledges the value that participating in a life and study skills course has for all new students. Many schools require that certain populations take this course. Some offer it only to honors students or to those students who are accepted provisionally or have low scores on entrance exams, SATs, or ACTs. Some require all developmental students to take this course. Be clear about who will be in your classes; this knowledge will assist you in writing a clear purpose statement and in stating the objectives for your course.

Whether you have heterogeneous or homogeneous groups, be sensitive to the needs and concerns of your students and consider how to involve them effectively in your classes.

Adapting to the Culture of Higher Education

Even though the average age of students is older than it once was, many students still go directly from high school to college. They enter higher education with no idea of the changes in expectations from high school classrooms to the college environment. As you think about creating the future of college survival courses, consider the following student populations that you list below. Consider the special support services these students will require as well as the diverse gifts they will bring to your college community.

What are the changing demographics and students' issues represented at your college?

_____

_____

_____

_____

Writing a Purpose Statement

A written purpose is the foundation of your course and the yardstick you can use to measure its effectiveness. Recopying or rewriting the college survival course purpose statement in your own words can

Copyright © Houghton Mifflin Company. All rights reserved.

provide you with greater confidence and clarity of intention. Consider the following questions when authoring your course's purpose statement:

1. What is your college's mission statement? How will this course promote the attitudes, behaviors, and choices your graduates are expected to exhibit in the world?

_____

_____

_____

_____

2. What is the profile of the students your college or university serves? What distresses and delights you about your students? What are the very best qualities of your graduates?

_____

_____

_____

_____

3. What do your upper class students say they learned "the hard way" or wish they could have done differently as first-year students?

_____

_____

_____

_____

4. What do the first-year core curriculum faculty members say are the challenges that hamper first-year college survival in their academic discipline? How could this course prepare students for the differences between their secondary school experiences and the expectations of higher education?

_____

_____

_____

_____

5. What would you say to first-year students if you had one last lecture to give?

_____

_____

_____

6. How would you sequence the college survival course topics and experiences if the students were in your class only for the first six weeks of the term? (Note: The first six weeks are considered the most crucial period for new students, according to retention research. By the sixth week, if students do not experience a sense of belonging and find value in their courses, they often decide that they want to leave, even if they actually endure for the rest of the term.)

_____

_____

_____

_____

   Copyright © Houghton Mifflin Company. All rights reserved.

Sample Purpose Statements
and Course Titles

It is interesting how authoring a purpose statement reflects the values of the writer. The following are sample purpose statements that educators have written during this exercise at College Survival workshops or trainings.

The purpose of this professional seminar is to empower students to achieve peak performance at an academic, a personal, and a professional level through the use of proven educational and mental strategies.

The purpose of this course is to give students an opportunity to create and change their habits and vision to allow themselves to have a rich, full, and rewarding personal, scholastic, and professional life through the adoption of positive strategies and techniques.

The purpose of the freshman seminar is to create an environment for honors students that enables them to grow personally, academically, and professionally. Therefore, the course will stress growth and personal and interpersonal development and provide specific information about the college and higher education in general.

The purpose of the orientation course is to assist the undecided student in improving academic skills, choosing a career, and enjoying the college experience.

The mission of College Foundations is to help students develop the skills essential to becoming the best they can be in all areas of life.

To provide life skills for cadets/students to enable them to be successful (by their definition) in both college and their future careers, military or civilian.

The purpose of this course is to provide students with an opportunity to cultivate the skills, values, and attitudes necessary to become confident, capable students and contributing community members (or to enrich them academically, personally, and professionally).

The purpose of Student Learning Strategies is to create experiences for students that will assist them in developing values, skills, and techniques that will enrich them academically, professionally, and personally.

The purpose of this College Success Skills class is to provide the tools that enable and empower a person to become or improve as a student and to succeed in all areas of life as a caring, aware, and responsible human being.

The purpose of EDU 102 is to create an opportunity to expose students to academic and personal tools that will help them to enhance their strengths, to acknowledge and develop their weaknesses, and to learn to adopt the tools in such a way that they can be modified for lifelong learning (enhancement).

The purpose of this College Success Skills course is to provide students an opportunity to adopt techniques and strategies to enhance their success in school and in their jobs and their ability to contribute to the lives of others.

The purpose of BUS 105 is to facilitate and promote college survival—both academic and career successes. It is to serve as a "fertile ground" on which students have the opportunity to begin to sow the seeds of success by developing themselves personally, academically, and professionally.

Our mission is to empower and inspire students to be successful, by their standards, in their lives (personal and professional) and in their studies by learning strategies (styles, changing of habits, and so on) that they can immediately and continuously apply throughout life and that enable them to leave the course with confidence, enthusiasm, and a passion to succeed.

The purpose of SLS 1101 is to provide an opportunity to develop skills and manners that will lead to success academically and in other areas of life; in short, to become and remain a student.

Copyright © Houghton Mifflin Company. All rights reserved.

Refining Your Course Purpose

One purpose for a college survival course is to provide an opportunity for students to learn and to adopt methods to promote their achievements in school. Every lecture, exercise, guest speaker, conversation/sharing, or other activity done in class has this purpose. Reminding students of their own purpose for being in school helps them stay focused. Purpose gives meaning and importance to daily routines. Examining purposes and keeping them in mind support success.

The intention of a college survival course is made clear by closely examining its purpose. You can review the course's purpose with students by discussing each of the following key phrases.

Purpose—Everyone has untapped potential. Becoming a master student is a lifelong process. The purpose does not prescribe a final destination. Rather, it suggests a direction of growth and learning. It is impossible, for example, to arrive at a destination called "East." Traveling east makes more sense than reaching a goal called "East." Ask your students to explain why. We can use a purpose as we would use a direction on a compass—to continually monitor our progress.

Provide an opportunity—*The American Heritage Dictionary* defines the word *teach* as "to cause to learn." A cause is defined as a person or thing "responsible for an action or a result." Since each student is responsible for her own learning, no one else can be the source or cause of that learning, so we have an interesting dilemma. No one can cause another person's learning, and teaching is defined as causing another's learning. There is only one possible conclusion: Teaching is impossible. Don't be discouraged. Teaching as a profession is not in jeopardy. Even though teaching in this sense is impossible, teachers nevertheless have a challenging and useful job. They provide an opportunity for students to learn. They invite students to learn. Teachers can set the stage in the most effective way possible for learning to take place. They can also convey that the responsibility for learning rests with the students.

Learning, defined as "the act . . . of gaining knowledge or skill," is not only possible, it is the most natural act humans can perform. It begins before birth and continues throughout life. Teachers are responsible for providing an opportunity. Students are responsible for learning.

Learn and adopt—Knowing what is needed to be successful, however, is not enough. Students might know many of the strategies suggested and not use them. They might know which behaviors would promote their success and not adopt them. Unless strategies for success are put into action, they are useless. This course encourages students to learn and to adopt methods that will enable them to be successful in school. This activity often requires behavioral change. Selling students on the idea of changing their behavior is the ultimate challenge of this course. Shifts in attitudes, values, and beliefs accompany shifts in behavior.

Methods—Most of the course involves concrete techniques and specific strategies for success. Even the parts that are more philosophical in nature can be used as tools to generate a successful experience at school and beyond. See *Becoming a Master Student* for a discussion of the Power Process "Ideas are tools."

Successful in school—No one description of success is appropriate for everyone. People are different and so are their pictures of success. This course is not intended to promote success as defined by parents, teachers, or administrators. Success is defined individually by each unique student.

Being a successful student might expand easily and naturally into learning more general life skills and ensuring success later in life and in one's lifework.

Possible Course Titles

Academic Development Seminar
Academic Resources
Achieving Academic Success
Becoming a Lifelong Learner
Becoming a Master Student
Beyond Creativity

Career Development
College Learning Techniques
College Preparation
College Skills
College Success Skills
College Survival

Copyright © Houghton Mifflin Company. All rights reserved.

College Survival Seminar
College Survival Skills
College Survival: Soaring with the Eagles
College Survival Training
Communications
Developing Study Skills
Discovery and Experience Through
    Liberal Arts
Educational and Life Planning
Efficient Personal Study Skills
Freshman Foundations
Freshman Orientation
Freshman Seminar
Human Development
Human Potential
Interpersonal Relations
Introduction to College Study
Introduction to University Studies
Invitation to Success
Issues in College Life
Keys to Success
Learning Techniques
Life Enhancement
Life Learning Skills
Life Management Skills and College

Master Student
Mastering Skills for College Survival
Mastery Skills
New Student Seminar
Personal Awareness
Personal Study Efficiency
Planning for Academic Success
Practical Approaches to Efficient Study
Preparation Skills for College Success
Principles of Academic and Personal
    Development
Professional Development
Psychology of College Survival
Resources Development
Self-assessment Career Development
Strategies for Academic Excellence
Strategies for Success: Freshman Seminar
Student Mentor Program
Study Techniques
Surviving and Thriving in College
Take Charge of Your Learning
Transitions
University Experience
University 101
University Survival and Study Skills

Classroom Management and Troubleshooting

This section presents ideas for handling common problems that might surface for many teachers of college survival courses. These suggestions have worked for others. Nevertheless, your own intuition and creativity in handling classroom situations will be far more valuable than trying to copy someone else's style. As with everything in this manual, adapt and modify these suggestions to fit your needs and presentation style.

    Whatever your concern, please call a College Survival consultant at 800-528-8323. Consultants are higher education educators and/or administrators who enjoy the opportunity to strategize with you and co-create options.

Students Resist the Class

Sometimes students resist taking this course. This is especially true if the program is new, required, or perceived as developmental. Here are a few suggestions for dealing with resistance.

"Sell" the course—At the beginning of the class, "sell" the students on the benefits they will receive from the course. Talk about how you think it is valuable, what the school philosophy is, and what they can gain academically and personally.

Recognize room for improvement—Surprisingly, A students often seem to get the most out of college survival techniques and speak most highly of the course. They want to study more effectively in less time.

Copyright © Houghton Mifflin Company. All rights reserved.

Students who protest that they "made it through high school" probably have a lot of room for improvement. Those students who really are satisfied with their study techniques will find that learning about themselves, each other, school policies, and resources while participating in the course is a worthwhile benefit.

Point to transferability—Many of the techniques students learn in this class are the same ones that will help them build successful careers, form happy relationships, and improve the quality of their lives, regardless of their choices.

Distinguish between "liking" and "benefiting"—We don't always like that which benefits us. Most students find something to dislike about the class. At the same time, it is almost certain that there will be beneficial aspects. Even if students find only a few ideas that work for them, their performance can still improve significantly. Those who resist the class and allow what they don't like to keep them from realizing its benefits are cheating themselves.

Be firm—Be clear about the guidelines for your class. Tell the students what you expect. If, after you do your best to convince them of the advantages of participating in class, some students choose to disrupt class and ignore your guidelines, it is appropriate to ask them to leave. If they complain that the course is required, tell them that you will not allow disruptive behavior in your class and that they must follow the guidelines or they will have to leave and repeat the course another term or not graduate. There is no reason to allow disruptive behavior in your class.

Bring in a speaker—Ask an administrator to come to class and explain school policies and philosophies and the benefits of the course. When students see administrators supporting and participating in the class, they are more likely to do the same. Bring in course alumni to discuss how they benefited from the class and how they are currently using what they learned from it.

Collect and read anonymous evaluations—Ask students to answer several questions about their reactions to the course on two-part sheets of paper. Possible questions include "What is effective and what is ineffective about this class?" and "What would make this course more worthwhile for you?" Also ask students to describe which methods and strategies they have found to be helpful and which have not worked. Read both positive and negative comments. During the first few class sessions, you can use comments from students who took the course previously. Later, you can share comments from students currently enrolled.

Do your own evaluation—Step back and look at the course from the vantage point of a student. If you were a student in your class, would you be getting what you need to reach your goals? Are the lectures, exercises, and other classroom activities assisting students in mastering the course objectives as stated in the syllabus? After you have thoughtfully evaluated your course, be willing to change. Telling students about the results of your evaluation and the changes you will make models a powerful way of taking risks and learning from mistakes. If you conclude that you are doing a good job, continue with confidence. Your job is to provide an opportunity for students to teach themselves.

Few Students Read the Text

Test over the reading—The text is designed to give students the content of the course. If they don't read and use the book, they aren't getting the most value for their money. Giving quizzes in class over the assigned material will encourage reading.

Collect the quizzes—The quizzes and/or the quiz answers can be removed from the text. The process of writing quiz answers will be beneficial, even if the student only paraphrases the answers from the articles, the back of the book, or another student's work.

When students know that quizzes will have to be removed from the text and turned in, they are more likely to read actively and invest more energy in learning the material. They will also realize that they are expected to participate actively with the text. This includes removing and reinserting pages, writing in the margins, and doing the exercises. Using the text in these ways will increase the book's value for the students.

Copyright © Houghton Mifflin Company. All rights reserved.

Collect exercises and Journal Entries—When you give a reading assignment, tell students that you will collect one of the exercises in the text. Don't tell them which one. Because the students won't know which exercise you will ask for, they might be more motivated to complete all of them.

Some of the exercises request absolute honesty from students. If students suspect you will choose one of these exercises, they might not participate with the fullest level of personal integrity. You can tell students which exercises you definitely will *not* collect and why (which will likely pique their curiosity).

Ask quiz questions about the exercises and Journal Entries—Whether you collect exercises and Journal Entries or not, ask questions about them on your quizzes. If students know that they will be asked about the exercises and Journal Entries, they are more likely to complete them. Questions could be about students' personal discoveries and possible applications of what they have learned.

Allow students to teach—Teaching is one of the best ways to learn. Since most students are not confident enough in their speaking skills to stand up and "wing it," they will probably be motivated to prepare before they teach. Consequently, they will learn the material they are about to present. Students might also gain an appreciation for your efforts as an instructor.

Tailor the text—Select the articles and exercises most appropriate for your class. Keep your course purpose and objectives in mind when you decide what to keep and what to omit.

Students Say They Don't Need This Course

Agree with them—Acknowledge that students probably already know a great deal about being successful. Also acknowledge that there is always room for improvement. Ask students to consider the possibility that learning and adopting a few truly effective strategies can save them time, improve their performance, and make a significant difference in the quality of their school experiences.

Use course alumni as guest speakers—Students listen attentively to other students. You can often find alumni who resisted the course at first and later on became great proponents of it.

Celebrate small achievements—Very few of us ever have an opportunity to improve 100 percent. Suggest that improving 1 percent in a hundred different ways can accomplish an equally impressive result.

Several Students Are Failing

Hold a conference—Set aside time for a face-to-face talk about your expectations and the student's expectations for the class. There might be confusion about what is required. Often homework is neglected due to other difficulties in a student's life. A committed listener is sometimes all that is needed. If more help with assignments is appropriate, refer students to other resources.

Remind students—Review the requirements for passing the course and remind students about their contracts, if they made them. Procrastination can be deadly—even for A students.

Detach—Allow students to make their own decisions and to accept the consequences. Students should take responsibility for their choices. Beware of your desire to take care of them. Some students will choose to fail. Failing this class can be a valuable experience. If a student fails accounting, she can say, "I never was very good at math." If she fails creative writing, she might complain, "I had a poor second-grade teacher." However, if she fails a college survival course, she has the opportunity to admit that she simply chose to fail.

Examine your standards—Determine whether or not you have set realistic goals for the class. If 50 percent of the class is not comprehending the material, examine your teaching methods, testing style, and classroom atmosphere. Feedback from students in the form of anonymous evaluations can be helpful, even if a little painful. If you decide that the way you are handling the class is satisfactory (remember, there is always room for improvement), then detach. Having students who choose to fail your class does not make you a bad person or a poor teacher.

Copyright © Houghton Mifflin Company. All rights reserved.

Students Feel Insulted

Acknowledge their skills—Students possess valuable life experiences that can assist them in school. This class can help them translate and adapt those skills in ways that will promote their success.

Let them choose—Have students pick and choose what's important for them. Encourage them to use the content that is applicable to them.

Focus on special challenges—Different students face unique and different challenges. Define and discuss these challenges in class.

Students Seem to Dislike You

Don't jump to conclusions—Sometimes the most unresponsive-looking students are creating an incredible amount of value for themselves from the course materials.

Don't give up—Some students have a cool or tough act that takes a while to break through.

Don't take it personally—Of the more than five billion people in the world, some won't like you no matter what you do. Remember the distinction between "liking" and "benefiting." They don't have to like you to learn from you. Refer to the article "Create your instructor" in the text for a more complete discussion of this concept.

Remember your purpose—Your job is to promote college survival, not to win a popularity contest. Being the person who holds up a mirror of self-responsibility and holds students accountable is not always a popular role. Sometimes you must choose between being liked and doing your job.

Students Exhibit Disruptive Behaviors

Be clear about your rules—Set limits and enforce them. Consistency is important. Students sometimes test teachers to find out where the lines are drawn. A practice of enforcing the rules one day and letting them slide the next is confusing to students. Be explicit about your expectations and be consistent about applying the consequences for not following the rules.

Ask students to remember their purpose—Ask students to reflect on their reasons for being in school and what they hope to gain. Discuss side conversations and have students consider the costs and benefits of such behavior.

Give feedback—Use "I" messages to share your observations, feelings, thoughts, wants, and intentions about side conversations. The purpose is to communicate in a way that students understand, not to make them feel defensive.

Stop talking—Your silence is usually enough to get the students' attention.

Contract with students—Include "no side conversations" as one of the agreements in the "Agreements and the student agreement contract" exercise.

Don't allow it—Even though you might give students a choice on the "Agreement contract" exercise and some might not agree to stop having side conversations, you don't have to tolerate talking in your class. Decide on your policy ahead of time and state it. While you cannot physically stop side conversations, you can enforce consequences. One or two reminders will usually handle the problem. If this approach doesn't work, ask students who are disruptive to sit apart from each other. If class participation is part of a student's grade, points can be deducted for side conversations. If students continue to have side conversations, request that they leave the room. Students then know that if they choose to have side conversations, they are choosing to be dismissed from the classroom.

Claim your classroom space—Walk around the classroom as you present material. Standing next to students who are having side conversations as you continue to present material lets them know that side conversations are not acceptable in your class.

 Copyright © Houghton Mifflin Company. All rights reserved.

Establish guidelines for and reinforce acceptable behavior—Include on the syllabus a written statement of the kind of behavior that contributes to a productive learning environment.

Immediately engage the student—Speak the name of the disruptive student while asking her to contribute or respond to what is being presented or discussed in class at the time.

Document continued disruptions—Keep dated notes regarding a student's behavior and ask to meet with the student. Be ready to make a referral to counseling or student services, if it is appropriate.

Change testing conditions—Separate students. Have student assistants monitor the class during tests.

Allow students to work in teams—Working in teams encourages camaraderie and support groups. Students can study together, take the test together, and receive a group grade. You can design tests that require some group discussion and group decision making.

Students Do Not Participate

Review the advantages of full participation—Discuss what students will gain, what obstacles to their success they might overcome, and how each exercise relates to the purpose of the course. Ask them to consider how much more they learn when they risk feeling foolish.

Be structured—Give highly structured directions that lead students through exercises step by step. Sometimes having to discuss a topic with others or even having to choose a partner frightens students. Use specific directions such as: "In a moment stand up, walk around the room, and ask people when they were born. When you find someone born during the same month as you, find a place to sit down with that person. You can sit anywhere in the classroom. Then, exchange names and have a brief conversation. I will then give you the next directions. Now, stand up and pick a partner."

Demonstrate—Use volunteers or model what is expected. Demonstrate the whole exercise, if necessary, to clarify what it requires and to help students feel more comfortable with it.

Give them the choice—Students who choose not to participate have as much to learn about themselves as those who do take part. You can still ask students who do not participate to write Discovery Statements and Intention Statements about what they learned by not participating.

Students Do Not Attend Class

Call them—Be sure that your records include a telephone number or an address for each student. A contact works best if it is made in a completely nonthreatening way. Avoid being judgmental. The purpose of this course is to encourage each student to succeed according to her definition of success. Remind the student of your purpose and express your concern about her performance.

Invite them to contact you—Recommend that students stop by your office. An interested teacher is often all that is needed to get a student back on track.

Students Complain That They Don't Have Enough Time

Suggest the opposite—Tell students that they can't afford not to have time for the course work. Taking this course can dramatically improve their efficiency and therefore give them more time for other things.

Discuss the benefits—The benefits from this class will carry over into all of the students' other classes and into the rest of their lives. Investing their time and energy can pay off in higher grades, more efficient use of time and money, better relationships, and so on.

Give synergistic assignments—Design your assignments so that students can combine them with assignments for other classes. For example, have students use Muscle Reading for their history assignment. They could submit to you an outline, questions that they generated before they read the assignment, and the answers to those questions. They could also write an evaluation of the effectiveness of the strategy as an assignment.

Copyright © Houghton Mifflin Company. All rights reserved.

Students Complain That the Text Is Too Expensive

Encourage students to keep the text—Describe the text as an owner's manual for an expensive purchase called "education." Encourage students to keep the text after the course ends as a resource manual for the rest of their education. Writing a speech might not be a concern until their fourth term. If they still have the text, they can review the speechwriting suggestions then.

Consider the value of information—Even if students adopt only two or three ideas from the hundreds that are suggested in the text, those ideas can make a significant difference in their performance in school and beyond. The investment in improving their school performance and the resulting impact on the rest of their lives are far more valuable than the cost of the text.

Shop around—Bookstores have different percentages of markup. Alternatives to buying through the college bookstore might be available. Be sure to get permission from the appropriate people. You can also discuss the markup with your bookstore manager and request that the store maintain reasonable prices.

Compare prices—Compare the cost of *Becoming a Master Student* to the prices of similarly formatted books in other disciplines. Students will find this text competitively priced.

Encourage active participation—The value of the text is increased when students actively participate with it. Stress that *Becoming a Master Student* is a text. The assignments are not simply to "read" the chapters; rather, students are expected to "read and do" them. Be sure that exercises and quizzes are completed and turned in to you.

Make informed decisions—Find out the extent of the concerns about the text's price. Often a vocal minority gets more attention than the rest of the students. When you know the extent of the problem, you can make more effective decisions about how to handle it.

Offer scholarships—Create a scholarship fund for students with special needs. Direct students to financial resources that already exist or suggest other possibilities that they can explore.

Prioritize your lesson on managing money—Sometimes students who say they can't afford to purchase the text might be experiencing other financial problems. The suggestions in the Resources chapter can help students discover other places to find money. The exercises on the HMClassPrep CD-ROM can also help students improve their money management. Have students compare the cost of the text to the costs of other commonly purchased items and discuss the relative value of each to their lives and education.

Highlight benefits—Ask students to consider the impact the course can have on their success in school and, consequently, on their success in life. Generating a list of all of the benefits can help reinforce their decision to take the course. These lists can be offered to administrators to help expand the course and to give students credit for taking it.

Petition your school—Do public relations work for the course. Go through appropriate procedures and channels to express your thoughts about the importance of the course, what it has to offer students, and how the institution will benefit. Campaign for the course to be made available to everyone for credit so that there is a reward for students in addition to that of self-improvement.

Consider transcript credit—Credit can sometimes appear on the students' transcripts and not be applied toward their degrees or calculated into their GPAs. This can be a workable compromise for schools with complicated credit-granting policies.

Course Lacks Faculty and Administrative Support

Contact College Survival—College Survival can assist you in gaining faculty and administrative support for your course. Call 800-528-8323 and ask to speak with one of the educational consultants or to arrange an on-site training at your college.

Outline the benefits—Describe the expected results of the course to administrators. When a successful course is delivered, students, faculty, administrators, and staff all benefit. Call College Survival for a booklet entitled "Gaining Support for College Survival Courses."

 Copyright © Houghton Mifflin Company. All rights reserved.

Use past evaluations—Testimonials from students who have taken the class can help your colleagues see the benefits of this course. You can also videotape students discussing their reactions to the course. Administrators might be more willing to watch a short videotape than to read dozens of written evaluations. Another possibility is to summarize evaluations, quoting pertinent and typical comments.

Conference call—Set up a conference call with a consultant from College Survival. Invite anyone who might be interested in, involved with, or skeptical about the college survival course to participate.

Share retention figures—Tracking retention rates will supply the evidence you need to convince others about the value of the course. You can find ideas about maintaining retention figures in Part IV of this Course Manual.

Send letters—Send letters to all faculty, advisors, and administrators describing the course and its purpose. Invite anyone who is interested to sit in on a class or to be a guest speaker.

Offer workshops—Schedule workshops on course content. Many of your colleagues might be interested in time management, goal setting, interpersonal communications, or the Power Processes.

Instructor Has Little Time to Prepare

Sometimes the assignment to teach a college survival course is given only days before the course begins. This circumstance is unfortunate and ineffective, and not hopeless. Here are some suggestions that can help.

Seek assistance—Instructors who have taught the course before are often willing to assist you. Ask them to help you get started.

Use this Course Manual—Read Parts I and II of this Course Manual first to get the big picture. When you have more time, explore the rest of the manual to develop a more solid foundation from which to create a successful course.

Enlist student support—Ask students to help you prioritize what's important to them. See the exercise called "Co-creating a syllabus" on the HMClassPrep CD-ROM.

Do preventive work for next time—Describe the problems resulting from not having had sufficient preparation time. Point to the costs for students, for instructors, and for the institution itself. Request that future instructors be given enough time to prepare for this class. Stress that when the class is supported and delivered effectively, retention rates improve and everybody wins.

Call College Survival—The consultants at College Survival have dealt with almost every problem imaginable related to college survival courses. Whatever your situation, they are likely to have a variety of suggestions and/or resources to share. Call 800-528-8323.

Students Don't Enroll

Market the course—Use brochures, newspaper articles, letters to parents and spouses, T-shirts, orientation speeches, letters to advisors, letters to students, and posters to describe the benefits of the course.

Promoting the Course to Students
(College Survival, November 1994)

At a Student Success Course Workshop in Charleston, SC, participants conducted a brainstorm session on ways to promote a college survival course to students. They compiled the following list during the session as a springboard for creating other innovative ideas. Look through this list of ideas. What could you adopt or adapt to promote your course?

- Have the class create a mascot and a song.
- Use a hot air balloon to advertise the course.
- Publicize course results in faculty and student newspapers.
- Ask current students to write a newsletter article about the course for extra credit.

Copyright © Houghton Mifflin Company. All rights reserved.

- Feature the "master students" in the course in a newsletter or on a bulletin board.
- Have a bring-a-friend-to-class day.
- Send out course information with admissions packets.
- Give local store and restaurant discounts to students who take the course.
- Award a prize to the student who directs the most referrals to the course.
- Create a master students' club for course graduates.
- Give special T-shirts away to the graduates of the class.
- Have a lottery for a free book and tuition credit for those who register.
- Perform a skit at orientation about the course.
- Bake a cake for registration that looks like the text and says, "Have a piece of success."
- Have successful course graduates attend registration wearing a button or sign that identifies them.
- Preprint the course title and number on registration cards.

Enlist help—Enlist advisors, registration and admissions staff, and others to help promote the course to students.

Schedule the class at prime times—A class offered at 5:30 p.m. on Friday is not considered a viable option by many students. Request that your course be scheduled at a reasonable time.

There Is Too Much Material to Cover

Correct! *Becoming a Master Student* was not designed to offer a prescription on how to be successful. It covers a wide range of topics and contains hundreds of suggestions that require experimentation by individual students to discover what they need and what is effective for them.

Pick and choose—Don't cover it all. Select only those items that are most useful. Get students' input to help you prioritize. Covering the most important items in depth might be more useful than trying to present all the material.

Suggest keeping the text—Students can keep their texts throughout their college years. When challenges arise, they can refer to the book and discover techniques to employ as new coping strategies.

Grading This Course Is Difficult

Start with an A—Tell students they begin the term with an A and then tell them what they can do to keep it.

Keep it simple—Keep your grading system simple. If you don't grade all of the work, define the requirements for successful completion of the course.

Get students involved—Have students hand in a written evaluation of their own performance, giving themselves a grade based on the course requirements.

Devise a point system—Assign points to regularly scheduled activities, optional or flexible activities, and extra credit activities. Give students a grid to use for tracking points early in the class. This might help students stay on track and be less anxious about grades.

Copyright © Houghton Mifflin Company. All rights reserved.

PART II:
COURSE MODELS AND COURSE CONTENT
Customizing Your Course

This section can help you select topics to best fulfill your course purpose and to address the issues facing first-year students at your college. Many schools customize college survival courses to address one, two, or all three of the major themes in *Becoming a Master Student*:

1. **First Steps**—encourage students to examine their current skills and assess areas for potential growth. Such scrutiny offers students the chance for reflection, self-knowledge, and development.
2. **Academic skills** (time, memory, reading, notes, and tests)—provide students with the knowledge and opportunity to improve scholastic skills and use techniques necessary for success in their core curriculum courses.
3. **Life and workplace skills** (thinking, communicating, diversity, resources, and health)—present students with opportunities to practice healthy lifestyles, balance their resources of time and money, improve communication to enrich relationships, and prepare for their careers.

Teachers of different courses might establish a module, workshop, or seminar approach for teaching these areas in one semester or two semesters. While these are the primary themes of a college survival course, you will find that critical thinking, personal responsibility, integrity, and expanding the role of the scholar will also be incorporated into each of these areas. Your individual college or university will emphasize the goals of its mission statement and showcase the people and programs available to support its students during their transition to college life.

This section of the Course Manual provides an overview of the topics that you can include under the three themes of *Becoming a Master Student* and offers models to promote partnership in the learning process, methods of instruction, and enhancement activities. Most teachers and students benefit by having a clear sense of where they are going. This section will help you express the purpose and benefits of each of these three themes in your own words to engage your students' interest in establishing goals and achieving academic, personal, and career success.

An Involving Course Model

After you decide which areas/themes you will cover in your course, you can zero in on the specific topics and articles you want to teach. Many of the strategies presented within a single topic can be used with equal effectiveness in a variety of topic sequences. The HMClassPrep CD-ROM contains several ideas that can be used in any chapter and at any time. Keep in mind that these are only suggestions. As you design your course outline and prepare weekly or daily lesson plans, choose if, when, and where you will use these ideas.

The ideas on the HMClassPrep CD-ROM are structured in the following seven-part format for easier application to both the planning and teaching processes. The objective is to use varying modes of instruction in order to facilitate a course that accesses and maximizes each student's method of learning.

Lectures	20%
Exercises	20%
Conversations and sharing	20%
Guest speakers and videotapes	20%

Copyright © Houghton Mifflin Company. All rights reserved.

Quizzes and evaluations ⎫
Previews and reviews ⎬ 20%
Assignments ⎭

It is not always possible to include all parts in every class period. Each of the seven parts can usually be included at least once a week. Over the entire term, 20 percent of class time is recommended for lectures, 20 percent for exercises, 20 percent for guest speakers and videotapes, 20 percent for conversations and sharing, and the remaining 20 percent for previews and reviews, quizzes and evaluations, and giving assignments.

The course is most effective when the following guidelines are met:

- The course is offered for credit.
- Students spend at least 30 contact hours in class.
- The course is taught over time (spread out over an entire term rather than during one or two weeks).
- Teachers are notified at least one month in advance that they will be teaching the course.
- Teachers are personally interested in teaching this course.
- Retention data on entering first-term students is maintained.
- Weekly quizzes and evaluations are given.
- End-of-term course and teacher evaluations are completed.
- Course materials (the text *Becoming a Master Student*, this Course Manual, the HMClassPrep CD-ROM, videotapes, and the telephone number for support services 800-528-8323) are given to teachers at least one month before the beginning of the course.
- Teachers are aware of and use the toll-free telephone consultation services available from College Survival.
- Teachers schedule at least one hour of preparation time for each hour of class time.
- Teachers are trusted by students and have good rapport with them.
- Student performance is evaluated (on either a pass/fail or graded basis).
- A seven-part format is followed (that is, the course is taught with a balance among lectures, exercises, guest speakers and videotapes, conversations and sharing, quizzes and evaluations, previews and reviews, and assignments).
- Teachers assigned to teach the course are trusted and respected by the administration and other faculty.
- The class is required of all full-time students who have fewer than 20 transfer credits from another institution.

Offering a course with at least 30 contact hours gives students enough time to learn and adopt methods to be successful in school. They need this time to experiment with the methods and turn them into habits. If your course has fewer than 30 contact hours, here are some tips:

- Include only those topics that are most useful for your students. Use the results from the Discovery Wheel exercise in Chapter One to help you determine which areas to cover.
- Ask students to assist you in creating an outline for the class. Completing both the Discovery Wheel and the First Step exercises in Chapter One will help them decide what to include.
- The chapters and articles in *Becoming a Master Student* have been designed to stand alone. You can use only those parts of a chapter that are relevant and useful for your students.

The Learning Styles Inventory (LSI)

People are fascinated by why they do what they do—and students are no exception. Taking the Learning Styles Inventory (LSI) in Chapter One gives students a chance to increase their self-awareness as learners. For instance, why does Jason find Chemistry 101 exciting and engaging, and his roommate thinks it's the

   Copyright © Houghton Mifflin Company. All rights reserved.

dullest way possible to spend a Wednesday morning? Or why does Sara love to attend her American Studies class, and finds that reading the material to prepare for class puts her to sleep?

The LSI gives students a way to make sense of what they're experiencing in college. However, they'll need you to guide them through the process of taking, scoring, and interpreting the inventory.

- Consider how best to set the stage for your students. Students often report feeling overwhelmed when they are left on their own to take the LSI, score it, and read the interpretation of the material as part of covering Chapter One.
- Introduce the LSI and go over the directions with them. Consider walking students through the scoring process, or ask them to wait to score the inventory until they're in class with you.
- Guide them in using the interpretative material—help your students connect it with their experience. Doing so will pay big dividends. Your students will begin to understand why they make the choices that they do, and they'll be better partners in the learning process.
- Watch the videotape *The Learning Styles Inventory: A Tool for Teacher and Student Success* on your HMClassPrep CD-ROM, or call your College Survival consultant at 800-528-8323 to obtain a copy of the videotape.

As you teach, your students will be more aware of how you're involving them in various parts of the learning cycle. And they'll learn to work with you—when what you're doing matches their learning preferences, and also when you ask them to stretch.

Background about the LSI

Developed by Dr. David Kolb at Case Western Reserve University in Cleveland, Ohio, the LSI measures a learner's preferences for *perceiving* information (taking it in) and *processing* it (making sense of the information). When these preferences are plotted on two continuums, four unique styles or modes of learning are formed. Students find that while every individual is capable of employing all four styles or modes, each person has a "preferred" way of learning.

Perceiving

In considering how students perceive information, Kolb uses a continuum ranging from **concrete experience (CE)** to **abstract conceptualization (AC)**. Those who favor perception through concrete experience generally prefer to deal with situations in a very personal way. They perceive by sensing and feeling, often taking an intuitive approach to problems. They usually function well in unstructured situations.

Those who favor perception through abstract conceptualization generally prefer to think things through. They analyze, intellectualize, and construct abstract theories to understand their experiences. They take a scientific approach to problems and often function well in clearly defined, structured situations.

For example, a teacher conducts a "get acquainted" exercise, asking students to walk around the room to introduce themselves and interview other students. Those who lean toward concrete experience are likely to be very comfortable with random mingling. Students who lean toward abstract conceptualization are more likely to prefer a set of well-defined instructions, including a specific set of questions to ask when interviewing other students. They might be uncomfortable during this exercise.

Processing

In considering how students process information, Kolb uses a continuum ranging from **active experimentation (AE)** to **reflective observation (RO)**. Those who favor processing new information through active experimentation generally prefer to jump in and start doing things. They immediately look for practical applications of what they have learned. They generally do not mind taking risks and are results oriented.

Those who favor processing information through reflective observation usually prefer to watch and ponder what is going on. They are generally interested in understanding a situation through careful observation. They are often capable of seeing several different points of view and can generate many ideas about how something happens. They are more likely to value patience and sound judgment.

In the "get acquainted" exercise previously mentioned, the students leaning toward active experimentation would begin immediately. They might value meeting as many people as possible and will generally

Copyright © Houghton Mifflin Company. All rights reserved.

leave a lasting impression on those they meet. Those who lean toward reflective observation might be slow to begin and are more likely to reflect on the meaning of the exercise and to form opinions about its utility.

Visualizing Learning Styles

Kolb depicts the relationship between how we perceive and how we process information by illustrating the processes on intersecting continuums. The vertical perception continuum ranges from **concrete experience (CE)** on the top to **abstract conceptualization (AC)** on the bottom. The horizontal processing continuum ranges from **active experimentation (AE)** on the left to **reflective observation (RO)** on the right.

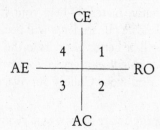

When the continuums are overlaid, unique styles or "modes" of learning are formed:
- Mode 1 (Why?)
- Mode 2 (What?)
- Mode 3 (How?)
- Mode 4 (What if?)

The labeling of the quadrants is useful only to help identify kinds of awareness. *No one mode or style is any better or more effective than another.* Individuals will generally have a preference for a particular mode, given the learning situations and environmental factors they encounter. Additionally, it is important to remember that every individual is a combination of all four styles. Following is a brief description of each quadrant.

- Mode 1 (Why?) learners combine the learning processes of concrete experience and reflective observation. People with this learning style are best at viewing concrete situations from many different points of view. Their approach to situations is to observe rather than to take action. Those with this learning style might enjoy situations that call for generating a wide range of ideas, as in brainstorming sessions. These learners probably have broad cultural interests and like to gather information. The imaginative ability and sensitivity to feelings characteristic of this mode are needed for effectiveness in arts, entertainment, and service careers.

- Mode 2 (What?) learners combine the learning processes of abstract conceptualization and reflective observation. People with this learning style are best at understanding a wide range of information and putting it into concise, logical form. Those with this learning style are probably less focused on people and more interested in abstract ideas and concepts. Generally, people with this learning style find it more important that a theory have logical soundness than practical value. This learning style is important for effectiveness in information and science careers.

- Mode 3 (How?) learners combine the learning processes of abstract conceptualization and active experimentation. People with this learning style are best at finding practical uses for ideas and theories. Those with this learning style have problems and make decisions based on finding solutions to questions or problems. These learners would rather deal with technical tasks and problems than with social and interpersonal issues. These learning skills are important for effectiveness in specialist and technology careers.

- Mode 4 (What if?) learners combine the learning processes of concrete experience and active experimentation. People with this learning style have the ability to learn primarily from hands-on experience. Those with this learning style probably enjoy carrying out plans and involving themselves in new and challenging experiences. Their tendency might be to act on "gut" feelings

   Copyright © Houghton Mifflin Company. All rights reserved.

rather than on logical analysis. In solving problems, they might rely more heavily on people for information than on their own technical analysis. This learning style is important for effectiveness in action-oriented careers such as marketing or sales.

The Importance of Understanding Your Learning Style

The ability to learn is the most important skill a person can possess. We are continually confronted with new experiences or learning situations in life, in our careers, and on the job. In order to be an effective learner, we have to shift from getting involved (CE), to listening (RO), to creating an idea (AC), to making decisions (AE). As an adult, you have probably become better at some of these learning skills than others. You tend to rely on some skills and steps in the learning process more than on others. As a result, you have developed a learning style.

Understanding your own learning style helps you become aware of your strengths in some aspects of the learning cycle, and you can help your students do the same. One way you can improve your learning effectiveness is to use those strengths when you are called upon to learn. More importantly, you can increase your effectiveness as a learner by improving your use of the steps you underutilize.

The following chart identifies the characteristics of each learning style and includes suggestions for further improvement.

MODE 4
Strengths:
  Getting things done
  Leadership
  Risk taking

Too much:
  Trivial improvements
  Meaningless activity
Areas needing focus:
  Work not completed on time
  Impractical plans
  Energies not directed toward goals
To develop your Mode 4 learning
  skills, practice:
  Committing yourself to objectives
  Seeking new opportunities
  Influencing and leading others
  Being personally involved
  Dealing with people

MODE 3
Strengths:
  Problem solving
  Decision making
  Deductive reasoning
  Defining problems
Too much:
  Solving the wrong problem
  Hasty decision making
Areas needing focus:
  Lack of focus
  No shifting of ideas/mistakes
  Scattered thoughts

MODE 1
Strengths:
  Imaginative ability
  Understanding people
  Recognizing problems
  Brainstorming

Too much:
  Paralyzed by choices
  Can't make decisions
Areas needing focus:
  Can't recognize problems

To develop your Mode 1 learning
  skills, practice:
  Being sensitive to people's feelings
  Being sensitive to values
  Listening with an open mind
  Imagining the implications of uncertain
    situations

MODE 2
Strengths:
  Planning
  Creating models
  Defining problems
  Developing theories
Too much:
  Castles in the air
  No practical application
Areas needing focus:
  Unable to learn from _____
  No sound basis for work
  No systematic approach

Copyright © Houghton Mifflin Company. All rights reserved.

To develop your Mode 3 learning skills, practice:

Creating new ways of thinking and doing
Experimenting with new ideas
Choosing the best solution
Setting goals
Making decisions

To develop your Mode 2 learning skills, practice:

Organizing information
Building conceptual models
Testing theories and ideas
Designing experiments
Analyzing quantitative data

Improving Learning and Problem-Solving Skills

Students can improve their ability to learn and solve problems in three ways:

1. Develop learning and work relationships with people whose learning strengths and weaknesses are the opposite of theirs.
2. Improve the fit between their learning style strengths and the kinds of learning and problem-solving experiences they face.
3. Practice and develop learning skills in their areas of weaknesses.

First strategy—Develop supportive relationships. This is the easiest way to improve learning skills. It is important to recognize one's own learning style strengths and build on them. At the same time, it is important to value other people's different learning styles. Also, students should not assume that they have to solve problems alone. Learning power is increased by working with others. Although students might be drawn to people who have similar learning skills, they'll learn more and experience the learning cycle more fully with friends and coworkers who have opposite learning skills.

How? If someone has an abstract learning style, such as Mode 3, he can learn to communicate ideas more effectively by associating with those who are more concrete and people oriented, such as learners who prefer Mode 1. A person with a more reflective style can benefit from observing the risk taking and active experimentation of people who are more active, such as learners who prefer Mode 4.

Second strategy—Improve the match or fit between a student's learning style and his life situation. This is a more difficult way to achieve better learning performance and life satisfaction.

How? There are a number of ways to do this. For some people, this might mean a change of career or job to enter a new field where they feel more comfortable with the values and skills required of them. Most people, however, can improve the match between their learning style and their tasks by reorganizing their priorities and activities. They can concentrate on those tasks and activities that lie in their areas of learning strength and rely on other people's help in areas of learning weakness.

Third strategy—Become a flexible learner. Students can do this by strengthening the learning skills in which they are weak. This strategy is the most challenging and is also the most rewarding. By becoming flexible, students will be able to cope with problems of all kinds, and they will be more adaptable in changing situations. Because this strategy is more difficult, it involves more time and tolerance for mistakes and failures.

How? First, develop a long-term plan. Look for improvements and payoffs over months and years, rather than right now. Next, look for safe opportunities to practice new skills. Find situations that can test new skills and will not punish you for failure. Lastly, reward yourself. Becoming a flexible learner is hard work.

Learning Styles and Teaching Strategies

Chapter One of *Becoming a Master Student* provides detailed descriptions of each of the four learning modes and cautions that no one style is better than another. Knowing one's preferences helps students understand why some parts of the learning process are interesting to them and why they like certain types of class activities more than others.

Students can use their understanding of learning styles to make choices that support their academic progress. They can learn to consider these questions:

 Copyright © Houghton Mifflin Company. All rights reserved.

- What does this learning situation involve?
- What will I need to do in order to understand the concept?
- How is this learning meaningful to me?

Integrating knowledge of learning styles into the curriculum can help teachers design a course that promotes success for all students. Knowing students' preferences, we can provide an opportunity for everyone to get involved in the learning process. As we choose our teaching methods to address various preferences at different points in the course, we meet different students' needs. Students in our classes typically represent all four styles of learning, so some students will sometimes find a good fit with what we're doing, and at other times they'll need to stretch beyond their preferences. Yet teachers can recognize the distinct approach that each learner brings to the curriculum and understand the process that learning involves.

Acknowledging learning styles lets teachers shift their energy from professing to facilitating. Rather than focus on the transfer of knowledge, we can use feedback about our students' learning to inform our teaching. Students come to realize that their interactions shape what happens in the classroom, and, rather than being passive recipients of an education, they become active participants in constructing their learning experience. Working together, teachers and students create an environment that promotes success.

Below are some specific strategies for using information on students' learning preferences. Consider using or adapting the ones that fit your situation best.

Review student profiles—Knowing the learning profiles of your students can help you identify activities that they will find most enjoyable and least enjoyable. This information can be useful during course planning. At the same time, avoid teaching only to student profiles. Encourage students to move through all four modes of learning.

Challenge students' excuses based on learning profiles—If students struggle with learning, they might blame this fact on teachers or on programs that do not match their learning styles. In response, you can challenge students to continue taking responsibility for their education. Point out that low performance during certain aspects of the learning cycle is OK. Also remind students that with practice they can develop skills across all modes of learning.

Use profiles to recognize when students struggle with learning—For example, students who have difficulty with Mode 1 might be those who are primarily interested in using information. These students could look bored, be eager to move on to hands-on activities, or point out that they are not in school to "have fun." They're not very interested in seeing the big picture or knowing why a particular topic is part of the curriculum. They're more interested in "how" than in "why."

Students who struggle with Mode 2 could have a difficult time with lectures or longer reading assignments. These students might find lectures dull or lose interest in texts that summarize factual material. They might feel overwhelmed with the details that you're providing, and wish that they could try out the concepts in their own settings rather than just talk about them in the abstract. They're more interested in "what if" than "what."

Students who have difficulty with Mode 3 might be those who are primarily interested in finding the rationale for learning new material or for finding out how the new topic fits into the scheme of things. They might not be so interested in using the material; they'd rather figure out how it fits in to what they already know about a concept. They're more interested in "why" than "how."

Students who struggle with Mode 4 are often primarily interested in covering more content rather than applying what they've already learned to new situations. Finding new ways to apply what they've already learned or to integrate their learning into different settings does not intrigue them. They'd rather know "what" than "what if."

Use profiles to help students get beyond struggling—Tailor your teaching strategies to the following four key questions, or modes, of learning.

1. **Why?** To support Mode 1, explain or demonstrate the importance of new learning. Let students experience the connection between what you are teaching and their current lives. Remember that

Copyright © Houghton Mifflin Company. All rights reserved.

students who favor this mode ask "Why?": "Why do I need to know this information? Why is this information important in my life? Why should I learn what you are teaching me?" If you can answer these questions when you begin teaching a new unit or concept, you can help students move through this stage successfully.

2. **What?** To support Mode 2, focus on the concepts and strategies that are most important. At this stage you might increase your effectiveness by choosing not to cover all of the material in a chapter or content area. Give highest priority to those topics that you want students to practice as a means to understanding. For example, you could assign only specific parts of a chapter or book.

3. **How?** To support Mode 3, allow time for students to experiment with, practice, and apply what you present. To fully understand what they're learning, students can conduct experiments, do projects, complete homework, create presentations, conduct research, tabulate findings, or even write a rap song that summarizes key concepts. Such activities provide an opportunity for students to internalize their learning through hands-on practice.

4. **What if?** To support Mode 4, allow students to demonstrate an understanding of what they've learned. This is a time for students to teach what they have learned to someone else, present findings from their research, report results from their experiments, demonstrate how their projects work, or perform the rap song that they wrote. You can use such activities to conclude a unit and assess student learning.

Encourage students to tolerate discomfort. When students struggle during a particular style of learning, remind them that the learning cycle includes all four modes. Also point out that neglecting any of the modes or moving too quickly through them can interrupt learning. Encourage students to endure discomfort and to accept it as a natural part of the learning process.

Avoid grouping students by learning profiles. If you do any grouping based on them, then create groups of students with differing profiles. Participating in a mixed group encourages students to develop skills in all areas of the learning cycle.

Explain how *Becoming a Master Student* can help students move through the learning cycle.

- At the beginning of each chapter, students will find a Journal Entry that asks them to connect the chapter content to their previous learning and experience (Mode 1: Why?).
- The body of each chapter offers ideas, information, and suggestions that can help students succeed in school (Mode 2: What?).
- Exercises throughout each chapter allow students to experiment with ideas and apply new skills (Mode 3: How?).
- The Learning Styles Application section at the end of each chapter includes four items to help students integrate the chapter content with their own lives (Mode 4: What if?).

Lesson Plans

Writing lesson plans around the cycle of learning is a method of teaching that reaches students with different learning styles. Using Kolb's learning styles model, the cycle begins with a concrete experience of a learning event or experience. Students reflect on this learning event, then create concepts from the event, and finally actively experiment or try out the learning event. This cyclical approach provides all learners with an opportunity to demonstrate their most developed skills at least 25 percent of the time. This also means that they will struggle some of the time and will have opportunities to learn new skills.

- **Mode 1 of the learning process**—combining concrete experience with reflective observation. Your lesson plan begins by laying the groundwork or establishing the context for what is to come. Talk about the content in general terms while giving many concrete "daily life" examples. The purpose of using such examples is to help students connect the new content with something they have already experienced, thus making the content more meaningful. Discussion time can be useful for encouraging students to learn more.
- **Mode 2 of the learning process**—combining reflective observation and abstract conceptualization. Now begin to lecture or provide the specific content of the lesson plan. This is when stu-

 Copyright © Houghton Mifflin Company. All rights reserved.

dents begin to comprehend the material and start creating concepts that form new building blocks of learning. They begin to put the pieces of the whole together as the facts are presented to them.

- **Mode 3 of the learning process**—combining abstract conceptualization and active experimentation. Your role now is to coach students' experimentation with the content. This is when students can determine whether the content will be useful to them. You can either do activities or exercises in the classroom or give outside assignments. These activities can be individualized or done in small groups. Students will be more active at this stage, and you will be coaching and facilitating.
- **Mode 4 of the learning process**—combining active experimentation and concrete experience. As students are actively experimenting with the content and discovering its utility in their lives, you can help them evaluate their results. At this stage, students integrate the content into their behavior and add something of themselves to it. In other words, they can now talk about the content in general terms and provide several "daily life" concrete examples of their own.

All learners have certain skills that assist or augment their ability to be successful in the classroom. Following is a list of activities that best facilitate each mode of learning. You can check your lesson plans to see if they include options, activities, and approaches that provide all learners with the opportunity to excel in your class.

Preferred Learning Activities

Mode 1 Learners
  Motivational stories
  Journal writing
  Simulations
  Subjective tests
  Group problem solving
  Socratic lecture
  Role playing

Mode 2 Learners
  Formal lectures
  Library searches
  Textbook reading
  Objective tests
  Problem solving by instructor
  Lectures with visual aids
  Independent research

Mode 3 Learners
  Homework problems
  Lectures with demonstrations
  Guided labs
  Objective tests
  Example problems worked by students
  Computer-aided instruction
  Individual reports

Mode 4 Learners
  Open-ended problems
  Quality circles
  Open-ended labs
  Subjective tests
  Problems prepared by students
  Student lectures
  Student presentations

A lesson plan for teaching time management follows, noting the preferred learning activities of the four learners' styles.

Mode 1 Learners

Learners' Goal: making a personal connection with the content

- Ask questions such as: "Have you ever needed more time to do all that you wanted to do? Would you like to know how to get more done in less time?"
- Role-play situations from your own life or from your students' lives to illustrate how you or they currently manage time.
- Ask students to write Discovery and Intention Statements about their use of time (to take a First Step about time).
- Ask students to write a response paper on "If I had all the time in the world, I would. . . ."

Copyright © Houghton Mifflin Company. All rights reserved.

Mode 2 Learners

Learners' Goal: gathering information about various systems of time management

- Ask students to discuss in small groups their current methods of managing time (both positive and negative) and to list all of the methods.
- Next, reconvene the class as a large group and share all of the methods that students use to manage time.
- Give this assignment: "Monitor your time for one time period (day, weekend, week), using any method you prefer, and log your activities."
- Teach concepts of time management from *Becoming a Master Student*: the Time Monitor/Time Plan, 25 ways to get the most out of now, and the seven-day antiprocrastination plan.

Mode 3 Learners

Learners' Goals: learning new concepts and applying them

- Continue teaching concepts such as the ABC daily to-do's priority system and goal setting.
- Complete this in-class exercise: "Now that you have monitored your time and have learned some new concepts and strategies, plan and monitor your next day, weekend, or week."
- Discuss (in small groups and as a large group) the discoveries students made after completing this exercise.

Mode 4 Learners

Learners' Goals: refining the applications and applying the learning

- Present minilectures on the Power Process "Be here now," goal setting, and Master Student Malcolm X.
- Ask students to write about their goals (academic, personal, and career).
- Ask students to role-play, make posters, or use music to demonstrate effective time-management skills.
- Ask students to write themselves a letter about their commitment to use more effective time-management techniques; place it in a self-addressed, stamped envelope; and hand it in. Mail these letters back to students in six months.
- Ask students to begin teaching to fellow students, family, and friends what they have learned about time management.

Conclusion

Kolb's model is one of many different ways to approach learning styles. It is important to be aware of the wide variety of factors that influence a particular learning style preference. These include modes of perception or modalities (visual, auditory, and kinesthetic) and environmental factors (room lighting, temperature, sound, and time of day).

Learning style modalities

The following are tips adapted from the philosophy of neuro-linguistic programming (NLP) for using modalities (auditory, visual, or kinesthetic) in the classroom.

Auditory learners

Tips:
   Natural listeners
   Speak more slowly than visual learners do
   Speak in a monotone

Favorite expressions:
   "I hear that."
   "That rings a bell."
   "Well informed."
   "To tell the truth."
   Quote other people: "He said . . ."

   Copyright © Houghton Mifflin Company. All rights reserved.

Learn by:
  Listening and verbalizing
  Using songs or rhythms
  Oral directions
  Rhymes
  Listening in the classroom
Teaching strategy:
  Take your time.
  Pay attention to sounding good.
  Plan and deliver an organized conversation.

Visual learners
Tips:
  Fast-talking
  Impatient
  Often interrupt
Favorite expressions:
  "I can picture that."
  "It appears that . . ."
  "It's not yet clear."
  "We see eye to eye on that."
Learn by:
  Seeing and imaging
  Using colors
  Using images, shapes, drawings, paintings
  Sculpting in the classroom
Teaching strategy:
  "Show" them things.
  Paint mental pictures.
  Use references and examples.
  Make reports and charts look good.

Kinesthetic learners (includes tactile or touch learners)
Tips:
  Slowest talkers of all
  Slow to make decisions
Favorite expressions:
  "I've got a feel for it."
  "I grasp your point."
  "It boils down to . . . "
  "Sensitive."
  "Motivate."
Learn by:
  Doing and manipulating
  Using body movements, dance, gesturing
  Physical actions in the classroom
Teaching strategy:
  Walk them through everything.
  They will need a hands-on demonstration.
  Engage their emotions.

Copyright © Houghton Mifflin Company. All rights reserved.

Lectures

It is difficult for most instructors to limit lectures to 20 percent of class time. Even when we know that lecturing is not the most effective teaching tool, we might be influenced by our own experiences as students and by the joy of being "on stage." Also, for some teachers, lecturing is far easier than attempting to get students to participate more actively in the class. In order to maximize the effectiveness of lectures and to avoid reliance on them, keep the following objectives in mind:

- Highlight material for students and encourage them to discover the content.
- Draw relationships among topics in the areas of academic and workplace skills.
- Explain the transferability of skills to other disciplines.
- Address predictable student crisis phases before they occur.
- For a "last lecture," decide what you most want to say to students completing your course.

Allow students to learn the basic content of the class from the text. Lectures can then be used to re-emphasize and clarify content, or to introduce new or supplemental material.

Give lectures over areas in which you have special skills and in which the students show interest. For instance, you might be an armchair specialist in nutrition and cognizant of how nutrition, food sensitivities, and vitamins affect academic performance. If so, a lecture about what you know might be entertaining and educational. Perhaps you were a professional speechwriter for ten years prior to your teaching career. You might want to spend more time and energy on the Reading or Notes chapters. Your enthusiasm for a subject that engages you will be contagious and in turn can help keep students' interest high.

Lecturing for re-emphasis can be tricky because students don't want to be treated as if they aren't smart enough to figure out what's in the book. However, when reading the text, students sometimes skim over or even totally dismiss important concepts and techniques without a second thought. Lecturing about critical ideas is one way to encourage that second thought. Often it is sufficient to say, "Yes, the nine steps of Muscle Reading seem like a lot of work, and I want to discuss them with you briefly because I am convinced that they will save you hours of rereading time. I did a lot of rereading before tests when I was a student, and it wasn't any fun!" Using a personal example or story is a good way to re-emphasize an important point.

Selling the benefits of using the strategies presented in the text increases the likelihood that students will experiment with them. Lectures about how college survival skills can transfer to careers can make students aware of other applications for them. The Workplace Applications in the text will support this effort.

If students are confused about an idea or a technique, you might find it useful to give lectures to clarify material after quizzes or class discussions. These lectures might seem more like class discussions because you will need feedback to figure out what is confusing students and how you can best re-explain ideas to make them understandable.

In the "Lectures" sections throughout the HMClassPrep CD-ROM, you will find suggestions for various lectures appropriate for this course.

Exercises

This course is designed for active student participation. The more that students contribute to a class, the more likely that they are to benefit from it. Exercises encourage participation and increase the level of energy in the classroom. They also provide avenues toward values clarification, interaction with other students, and applying or experimenting with the tools and techniques presented.

There are many types of exercises in the text, on the web site, and on the HMClassPrep CD-ROM:

- Springboards to sharing
- Springboards to intimacy
- Encourage participation

Copyright © Houghton Mifflin Company. All rights reserved.

Other types of exercises include the following:
- Warm-ups (low stress) for conversations about course content
- Energizing
- Interactive exercises on the Web
- Building relationships
- Promoting self-discovery
- Values clarification
- Application of skills
- Evaluation of skills implementation
- Wrap-up (closure) activities and conversations about course content

Students are often reluctant to write on or remove pages from their texts. You can encourage students to participate actively with the text on the first day of class. Use Exercise #1: "Textbook reconnaissance." Have students complete the exercise, tear it out, and turn it in. This exercise will give you a sense of the more popular topics that you can emphasize during the course.

You can share the collected pages with the entire class. Then hand back the pages and show students how to reinsert them into the text. "Sell" students on the benefits of getting to know themselves and each other better. Structured exercises are a nonthreatening way to give students an opportunity to connect with each other. Having a supportive group of friends can be a key factor in college survival.

Many exercises provide opportunities for students to experiment in a safe environment. Students are being asked to try a variety of strategies, to see which ones work, and to adopt new behaviors. Exercises offer a chance to practice this experimental process with little risk. For example, it might be easier to adopt mind mapping as a regular habit if it is first practiced in an exercise.

The HMClassPrep CD-ROM describes many exercises and divides them into several groups: Warm-Ups, Building Relationships and Personal Discoveries, Applying the Skills, and Closures. Select appropriate exercises based on the purpose of your class and your students' needs. Just as you ask students to experiment with various techniques, you can also be willing to experiment with various exercises. Some are great. Some are better than others. And some might be disastrous. It all depends on what works for you and for your students.

Writing a Discovery Statement or an Intention Statement on two-part sheets after an exercise is a good way for students to clarify what they have learned about themselves. Even those who chose not to participate in the exercise can write about what they learned by *not* participating. Using two-part sheets allows students to keep a copy for their own reflection and to give you a copy for taking attendance and for learning more about them.

Guest Speakers and Videotapes

Guest speakers and the videotapes that accompany *Becoming a Master Student* can help you accomplish the following:
- Introduce students to campus and community resources and role models.
- Feature experts on the course content.
- Give students and instructors a change of pace.
- Showcase assistance available in the community and at the college.

Possible guest speaker formats include the following:
- Cameo appearances (15 minutes)
- Roundtable discussions with students
- Panel of speakers with moderator
- Videotapes of speakers to be shown to multiple sections of the course
- Speakers to answer any topic generated by students

Guest speakers serve several purposes. They provide variety, present important content, and raise student awareness about available resources. Guest speakers give both you and the students a break. They

Copyright © Houghton Mifflin Company. All rights reserved.

take the pressure off you for a short time and expose students to different presentation styles. If there are multiple sections of your course, you can videotape guest speakers and show the videotapes to all sections. Also consider combining sections and scheduling a guest speaker so that all students can hear him.

When you invite a guest speaker to your class, first describe the class to him. Tell him about the purpose of the class, what a "typical" student is like, and what topics you want him to address. For example, a loan officer or financial aid director can present ideas from the chapter on Resources (Chapter Ten), plus any of his own thoughts for students. For the chapter on Health (Chapter Eleven), someone from Alcoholics Anonymous could discuss drugs and alcohol as well as share his personal experiences. You might want to allow the speaker to make up his own agenda after learning about the class.

Be assertive with your guest about what you would like him to accomplish, and be very specific about when his presentation will begin and how much time he can take. Ask him if you can signal when he has a few minutes left. Get his permission to cut him off if necessary. Some speakers might complain that the time is too short. Listen politely, apologize, and stand your ground. Remember that the purpose of inviting an archer is not to learn everything about archery. The purpose is to hear how the techniques of archery can be related to college survival.

Give your speaker directions about how to contact you and how to find his way around campus. A map might be useful. Also, ask him for some biographical information so you can introduce him effectively. Arranging for him to speak at the beginning of class or just after a break will give you time to meet and welcome him.

Speakers are an especially effective way to introduce students to campus and community resources. Even students who are from the area might not be aware of all of the services available to them. When selecting your speaker, keep your course purpose in mind.

Possible Guest Speakers

Librarian	Administrator
Tutor	Counselor
Placement director	Financial aid director
Student government director	Alcoholics and drug abuse counselor
Martial arts instructor	Mayor
Congressperson	Health professional
Public health official	Alumni
Professional athlete	Media personality/celebrity
Women Against Violence	Rape prevention worker
Child abuse counselor	Lawyer/judge
Banker	Business leader
Religious leader	Motivational speaker
Human resources representative	Scientist
Magician	Mothers Against Drunk Drivers
Career counselor	Aerobics instructor
Alternative health care professional	Ad agency executive
Law enforcement official	

Thank-You Notes

Finally, sending thank-you notes to speakers gives them positive reinforcement and demonstrates your students' appreciation. You can have students write their notes on two- or three-part paper. This practice enables you to include students' handwritten comments with your own note. Also include comments from quizzes and evaluations along with student reactions to the presentation. People enjoy feedback. It can motivate them to return for the next term. Following are two examples.

   Copyright © Houghton Mifflin Company. All rights reserved.

Sample Note #1

Dear Bill:

The students in Orientation class were eager to listen to alumni. They learned a lot from your presentation and were very positive about what you and your colleagues said.

I appreciate your willingness to take time from your workday to talk to our first-term students. At the end of the class, the students completed a quiz. The last question asked them to summarize what they heard you say and also to give their opinion of your presentation. The results were very positive. Here are some of their comments:

- I learned that I can quit feeling afraid and sorry for myself. They stressed the importance of sticking it out in college and how much you will need [college] later on. They stressed that no one is perfect, and they had fun in college, but still survived it. They also told how they had difficulties in classes and not to be ashamed to ask for help.
- The presentation was very interesting! They stressed that we should get involved in activities, clubs, and organizations.
- They gave an interesting presentation. I learned that even the most successful business people were not the best students in class.
- They really emphasized how important it is to learn all you can from your courses because it will help you in your working years.
- It made me feel secure and like I am going to make it.
- It was good inspiration to see students who have graduated and hear the kind of jobs they got. And that college can be fun, but that to achieve your goals, you have to work at it. I feel attending college was a good choice after all.
- They said that they had problems in classes, too, but they got through them. They were glad that they stuck college out.
- To me, the alumni told me to carry out my intentions. That may seem hard at first, but if I take on the right attitude, everything will work out. I am the creator of how well I succeed or do not succeed.
- I appreciated their presentation because it made me feel more secure in my decision to attend college.

The Orientation class meets every term, so I hope that we can do this again. You are an inspiration to the students. Thank you very much.

Sincerely,

Sample Note #2

Dear Alison:

Thank you for the time and energy that you spent in your demonstration of tae kwon-do. The response that you received from the students in the Orientation class was extremely positive. The advantage of your demonstrating tae kwon-do is that you also demonstrate the power of concentration and attending to only one activity at a time. In the class we talk about the virtue and usefulness of the concept "Be here now" and how discipline and persistence result in a successful academic career. All I can do is talk about it. You demonstrated it. Thank you.

I have next listed some quotes from a quiz/evaluation that I give the students at the end of every class. At the end of the class during which you demonstrated tae kwon-do, I asked them what their reaction to it was and how it relates to their success in college. Their responses included the following:

- The concentration involved in tae kwon-do could be used to thoroughly learn while you are reading. As a medical student, I was especially interested in hearing them explain how both the body and the mind are used to keep you from injury.
- I was thoroughly impressed by the tae kwon-do demonstration. The way it could relate to me in college is that by concentrating and covering the right tasks, I will be a specialist in school.

Copyright © Houghton Mifflin Company. All rights reserved.

- If you put your mind to it and give your all to anything, you can be as successful as the people demonstrating the tae kwon-do.
- I felt the demonstration was very interesting. It might relate to success in college by showing how persistence and attitude can help you learn.

I sincerely hope that we can do this again. The course is taught every term to first-term students. Thank you for your part.

Sincerely,

Conversations and Sharing

Conversations and sharing activities can include the following:
- Discovery of common concerns and celebrations
- Discovery of potential support groups by hearing about others' experiences
- "Dress rehearsal" for speaking in other classes
- "Thinking out loud" without debate

Alternate titles for these activities might invite greater participation:
- "Comparing notes"
- "Comments or questions"
- "Your turn"
- "Temperature-taking"
- "Open microphone"
- "Quotable quotations"

Students often say that this is the most valuable part of the class. It is a time when you turn the class content over to students, inviting their comments, observations, and discoveries. It is your turn to listen.

During conversations and sharing, students usually become more aware of similarities in their experiences. We often assume that no one shares our struggles, joys, troubles, questions, and concerns. Through conversations and sharing, students learn that others have the same fears, worries, strengths, and goals. They often discover that they are not alone in the challenges they face.

Students can begin to bond with other students and develop a personal support system. They can let their classmates know of their needs for childcare, rides, or help in certain subject areas. The more supportive relationships a student has, the more likely he will persist and achieve his educational goals.

Conversations and sharing also allow students to get to know the instructor and to voice opinions and concerns. Instructors who are informed about student needs and issues can be valuable advocates for them and can convey such concerns to the administration.

Having to speak in front of others is one of the strongest fears many of us have. Asking questions and participating in class discussions are important—and sometimes necessary—skills for students to develop. When a safe, structured environment has been created that promotes public speaking, students often report moving beyond their fears about speaking in class.

Setting the Stage for Conversations and Sharing
The following guidelines can help generate valuable experiences for students.

Model sharing—If you are willing to share parts of yourself that the average student does not see, you become more human in the eyes of your students. They will probably be more willing to share their insecurities, questions, dreams, achievements, or challenges with someone who is "real" to them.

Allow time for silence—Students often need some time to think before they know what they want to say or before they have the courage to say it. Allowing silence is essential in creating an atmosphere that says, "Your ideas are important to me. I am willing to let you have time to think so that I can hear what is hap-

   Copyright © Houghton Mifflin Company. All rights reserved.

pening with you." Explaining this concept to students is appropriate since they are probably not used to having instructors give them much time to think before they talk. The recommendation here is to wait 30 seconds or more before breaking the silence. Make sure your body language matches your message of inviting students to speak. Be relaxed. Since silence is uncomfortable for many people, this might take some practice.

Let the students know that the silence isn't intended to pressure anyone or make them feel guilty for not talking. Rather, it is to give them time to look inside themselves to see if they have anything to contribute or reveal.

Listen with detachment—Conversations and sharing is a time when students sometimes vent their frustrations and voice their complaints. If a student talks about something you might take personally, listen without rebuttal, justification, or defense. Frequently, just feeling safe and having someone listen attentively is solution enough for students.

Have "seeds" available—Sometimes inspirational stories, moving poems, meaningful songs, questions about the value of course material, or comments about school and community events trigger talking. Questions about current events, politics, environmental concerns, or even how college survival techniques have been useful in other areas of students' lives are appropriate. Anonymously reading Discovery and Intention Statements that you have collected from students often generates useful conversations. Two board games, Reunion and The Ungame, have hundreds of nonthreatening questions that can be used in the classroom without playing the actual games.

Here are some possible "seeds":
- What are your reactions to the film [or exercise or guest speaker]?
- Find two items in your purse, wallet, or pocket that are important to you. Talk about them.
- Which ideas or techniques from the book have you tried? Which ones worked? Which ones didn't work?
- What do you need from your family or friends to promote your success?
- How can the faculty or administration of the school promote your success?
- What are some of your obstacles to getting what you want from school?
- What exciting or interesting things are happening around the school or community?
- What interesting occurrence in your life would you like to talk about?
- Describe a time when you were successful.
- What advice would you give to a new student?

Change the physical environment—Sometimes a change in the physical of environment helps cue conversations or exercises. For example, have students pull their desks into a circle or semicircle, or have them all stand up or sit on the floor. Getting them out of their passive listening-to-a-lecture posture could encourage more receptivity and openness.

Structure the time—Try this technique developed by Virginia Satir, a world-renowned author, lecturer, and counselor. She calls it "Temperature Taking." Once during each class period, announce that it's time for Temperature Taking. This is an opportunity to find out what is going on with people in the room. It is when you listen to students in a loving, nonjudgmental way. List the following five items on the blackboard and then discuss each one. Give anyone in the room a chance to speak at each step of the way. If no one has a comment, move to the next item. If this exercise tends to take too long, set a time limit before you start. The five steps to guide the sharing are: (1) appreciations, (2) bugs, (3) puzzles, (4) new information, and (5) hopes and wishes.

When introducing the idea of Temperature Taking, let the students know the ground rules for each of the steps. The guideline for appreciations ("warm fuzzies") is that they be specific. Compliment the details of what you like rather than giving general praise.

Irritations are expressed during the second step, bugs. When complaining, a student must also present three possible solutions. The group can then offer additional solutions. Puzzles are questions; in this third step, the group is invited to give answers to the perplexed person or at least to describe ways to find an answer.

Copyright © Houghton Mifflin Company. All rights reserved.

Step four, new information, is the time to relate anything new that has happened. In step five, hopes and wishes are limited to those of the person speaking. This is not a time to wish someone else were different. The group is asked to do all it can do to make the person's wish come true.

Relax and have fun—This is a time when you can get to know the students in your class, and they can get to know you. It can be rewarding for everyone.

Discuss Guidelines for Conversations and Sharing

It is helpful to discuss the guidelines for conversations and sharing on the first or second day of class. It is important to let students know what you expect. Students are more willing to participate when the environment is safe, and knowing the ground rules increases their feelings of safety.

Any topic can be brought up during conversations and sharing. The suggested approach is holistic because all aspects of our lives are interrelated. An exciting or disturbing event in one area of a student's life will carry over into all other areas, even if only in a minor way. If you are uncomfortable about allowing certain subjects to be raised, you can restrict this guideline by directing the students to share anything related to school.

Confidentiality is essential in providing a safe atmosphere for sharing. Ask students to agree that anything discussed in the classroom during conversations and sharing stays there. This dictum cannot be enforced, yet it is important to request and emphasize it.

Sometimes students' comments about themselves, about you, about others, or about the institution will be negative. If the problem mentioned is about a specific person, request that no names be used. This policy can be useful for keeping this activity from turning into a mudslinging or person-bashing session.

Practice Listening for What's Really Going On

A particularly strong attack might be a way for a student to release frustrations occurring in another part of his life. If you suspect that a student is having serious difficulties, you can talk privately with him and then refer him to an appropriate resource.

Listening for the request implied or imbedded in a complaint can save a lot of frustration and move a student toward resolving an issue. Complaints alone often do not lead to resolutions.

Be detached—Being detached when listening to students facilitates your listening and, consequently, also facilitates the students' speaking. Detachment is especially helpful if the criticism is about you, the instructor. In this case, just listen and try to understand the student's point of view. Defending yourself could add to the problem. Listening in a way that makes the student feel he is being heard is often all that is needed to eliminate the problem.

Let students know that this is not a time to debate or to criticize what other people have said. To ensure that this guideline is followed, have students address all comments to the instructor or to the entire class. Imagine a reserved student finally gathering his courage to announce to you and the class that he is having a terrible time in algebra only to have a few people snicker or make wisecracks about his intelligence. He probably wouldn't open his mouth again.

Choose when to answer questions—Questions might not be answered immediately. Announce to students that if a question requires more than a short answer, you will write it down and respond to it later. Your purpose during conversations and sharing time is to listen and to receive student comments nonjudgmentally. Use active listening techniques to ensure that you are really understanding what students are trying to express.

Discussions that need more time can continue outside of class. If a student shares something in class and wants feedback or needs more time to talk, suggest that the student meet with you outside of class to continue your discussion. You can also refer students to the available campus and community resources.

Learn names—Ask students to begin by stating their names. This procedure makes it easier to remember names. When students know each other's names, the opportunities for networking outside of class increase.

 Copyright © Houghton Mifflin Company. All rights reserved.

Increasing Students' Participation in Classroom Conversations

Sometimes, even after allowing time for silence, the conversations and sharing portion of your class needs a boost. Here are some ideas.

Model—Modeling is a powerful tool. You can prompt sharing by disclosing something about yourself. By being open and candid, you demonstrate trust in your students, and they are likely to follow suit.

Limit conversations and sharing time—When students know that the time is limited, they might feel more urgency to speak what is on their minds. They might value the time more and choose to use it wisely.

Have a "problem box"—Invite everyone to write anonymously about areas of concerns, questions, beliefs, or whatever issues they would like to hear discussed. During each class period, you can select two or three written comments and discuss them as a group.

Brainstorm topics—Ask students to brainstorm possible topics that would be useful and appropriate to talk about during conversations and sharing.

Be aware of timing—Schedule conversations and sharing after an exercise when students are already in an active and participatory mode.

Decreasing Students' Participation in Classroom Conversations

Set a time limit—Structure conversations and sharing for a specified length of time during each class. Setting aside a part of every class period for students to say what's on their minds assures them that they will have an opportunity to participate. Ask for those who have never participated (or who do so infrequently) to please speak.

Limit subjects—If students are taking too much class time "sharing," then ask them to speak about matters related only to school. Or announce a "conversations and sharing subject" for the day.

Create small groups—Breaking the class into small discussion groups gives more students a chance to participate. Encourage those students with similar concerns or interests to get together after class and continue their discussions. This could facilitate the beginning of support groups and friendships that can help keep students on track in school.

Meet privately—There are usually some students who monopolize conversations. They might need a caring listener. You can spend time with such students or refer them to a counselor or peer advisor. If a student seems to monopolize the time for conversations and sharing, explain your concerns in private and ask him to examine his motivation for talking so much.

Quizzes and Evaluations

Quizzes and evaluations can help you accomplish the following:

- Emphasize the rigor of this and other college courses
- Provide feedback for instructor and student
- Encourage teaching toward objectives
- Facilitate practice and application of skills
- Provide information useful for improving the quality of the course

Quizzes provide feedback to instructors and students and are consistent with higher education curriculum design and practices. They are valuable in determining how students are comprehending, applying, and experiencing the material being presented in the course. Content-related questions can be balanced with questions asking students to give their affective reactions to the course. Quizzes can tell you which ideas need clarification, which techniques could use re-emphasis, and how the overall atmosphere and content of the class can be improved. Compliments and complaints can be passed along (anonymously, of course) to those administrators and staff members most involved in the areas discussed.

Copyright © Houghton Mifflin Company. All rights reserved.

If a large number of students miss a specific content question, consider reviewing that material in class. If students rave about a particular guest speaker, consider inviting him back again.

Quizzes can be short. Five or six questions take about 10 to 15 minutes to complete.

Generalizing about student reactions based on the comments of only a few is tempting and dangerous. Using quizzes and evaluations to find out exactly how many students think and feel can help you decide what adjustments, if any, to make.

Anonymous feedback from the quizzes can be given to the entire class. Sharing these concerns helps students realize they are not alone in the challenges they face. This approach also allows students to find out what their peers are thinking.

Quizzes do not have to be graded rigorously. The aim is to make certain that the students complete each question and that the answers are correct. When a student fails a quiz, you can request that he take it again. Quizzes are not intended to put another obstacle in students' educational lives. The intent of the entire course, including quizzes, is to promote student success.

If your class is graded on a "pass" or "no pass" basis, you can give a student who does not pass a quiz the chance to retake it. This helps to ensure that the student understands the content and gives him an opportunity to experience success.

Have students take the quiz on three-part carbonless paper. After completing the quiz and turning in the top sheet, students can look up the answers in the text and in their notes and grade their own papers. They can correct any questions they missed and receive one-half credit for each corrected answer. Then have them turn in the second, corrected sheet. This practice turns the quiz into a learning, as well as a feedback, tool. Important concepts are reinforced as the students review the text and their notes. Students also learn how complete and valuable their notes are.

In addition to evaluation questions on quizzes, periodic anonymous evaluations are a way for students to give honest appraisals of you and the course. This feedback can help you refine and improve the course. Sharing these evaluations with your administrators will give them direct input about the value of the class and indicate what modifications, if any, would be helpful.

Keep your records for each class for a few years—at least until the students involved have graduated. If passing this course is a requirement for graduation, you might be asked to explain a failing grade a few years from now.

Previews and Reviews

Previews and reviews can do the following:
- Set the stage for learning and application
- Advertise what will come next
- Anticipate students' objections and defuse resistance
- Use repetition to reinforce concepts
- Set the standards of high expectations and student involvement
- State questions for students to consider during lectures
- Help to identify immediate and longer-term benefits of the course content and process

Previews and reviews reinforce the spiral approach of the text. *Becoming a Master Student* makes frequent references to what is coming up and what has already been presented. Previewing a class sets the stage for learning and enhances interest. Reviews are an excellent way to refresh students' memories, improve recall, and assist students in focusing their attention.

Reviewing can include summarizing quiz results and evaluation answers. Tell the class how, in general, they performed on a quiz. Let them know their collective opinion from evaluation questions. Read selected Discovery or Intention Statements to give students a balanced overview of what others are learning and what goals they are setting. The Discovery and Intention Statements you read might be from the quizzes or from two-part sheets that you collected in class.

   Copyright © Houghton Mifflin Company. All rights reserved.

Assignments

Assignments can help achieve the following:
- Indicate application of concepts and suggestions
- Promote out-of-class discussion and application of skills
- Begin implementation of successful behaviors
- Alter, enhance, or refine habits for achieving personal and academic success
- Ensure that students will examine materials outside of class
- Advocate "knowing" skills and also putting them into practice

Because *Becoming a Master Student* is a text, special emphasis can be put on reading and completing exercises in the text. The text is the critical part of the course. It contains the nuts and bolts (academic skills and life and workplace skills). Requiring students to complete the text exercises as part of their homework assignments allows you to use class time to explore life and workplace skills: building relationships, clarifying values, applying concepts, exploring campus and community resources, and sharing personal and academic issues. If your class is geared mostly toward academic skills, this class time can be used to apply the techniques presented in the assignments to the students' general education course work.

Some exercises in the text might be more effectively done in class. Pick the ones you'd like to do during class time and exclude them from chapter homework assignments.

You can also limit the assignments required in a short course by assigning only selected articles, Journal Entries, critical thinking entries, Learning Styles Applications, and exercises.

Lesson Plans

Prior to each class, write your lesson plan and rehearse. Recognize the time limits and how quickly the minutes go by. Write down any announcements to be made, topics to be covered, assignments to be given, jokes or stories to be told, record-keeping procedures to be performed, answers to questions that have been asked in previous classes, or material to review before continuing. Make sure all of the material fits together. Review Part I of this Course Manual for more ideas for preparation and classroom management.

Make a list of all of the items you will need to take to the class and check them off as you gather them together. These might include handouts, chalk, markers, 3x5 cards, pencils, two-part exercise sheets, three-part quiz sheets, student comments from the exercise or quiz collected at the last class, lecture notes, audiovisual materials, papers to return, the class attendance list, and your grade book. Be sure you have arranged for the delivery of any equipment that you or your guest speaker will need. Note how much time you expect each part of your plan to take.

Teaching sometimes resembles a theater production because it requires a great deal of preparation and attention to detail. A detailed plan allows you to have confidence, especially when you decide to deviate from it. When something unexpected happens and you choose to take advantage of the circumstances, a detailed plan allows you to quickly reprioritize and return to your plan later. A sample lesson plan follows. Plan, rehearse, be flexible, and "break a leg."

College Survival—Day 1

8:00 a.m.	(3 minutes)	Welcome
8:03 a.m.	(15 minutes)	Power Process "Ideas are tools"
8:18 a.m.	(10 minutes)	Preview and "Textbook reconnaissance" exercise
8:28 a.m.	(12 minutes)	"Name tag" exercise
		Purpose
		Direction
		Experience
		Discussion

Copyright © Houghton Mifflin Company. All rights reserved.

8:40 a.m.	(30 minutes)	"Sell" class
		Letters to new students from previous students
		Dyad discussion
9:10 a.m.	(40 minutes)	"Agreement" exercise
		Put model on board.
		Post office hours and phone number.
		Give instructor's agreements next week.
		State expectations.
9:50 a.m.	(10 minutes)	Librarian
		(Remind class of library requirement)
		Assignment: Read and do Chapter One.
		Remember: Take a 10-minute break when appropriate.

Remember to bring to class:

Markers/chalk	*Additional reminders:*
5x7 cards	Sell the class.
Straight pins	Power Process "Ideas are tools"
Syllabus (50)	"Naming" exercise
32 crisp $1 bills	"Agreement" exercise
	Library assignment sheet

Lesson Planning Tools

There are many ways to approach planning your course. The following are a few strategies you can use to customize your course and to construct detailed class outlines.

3x5 Card Course Planning Strategy

The purpose of using 3x5 cards for goal setting is to help teachers "divide and conquer" goals that might be difficult to attain because they seem insurmountable. These can be long- or short-term goals. In this exercise, students break these goals into tasks that can be accomplished in an hour or less.

Part I—Each student will need a pack of 3x5 cards for this exercise. Briefly preview the directions. Brainstorm for three minutes. Tell them to think of all the things they would like to accomplish in their lives. Give these directions: Write each goal on a separate 3x5 card. Do this now. Take a few minutes and choose one of those goals—one that will take a long time to complete, such as writing a book. For the next five to eight minutes, brainstorm again. This time, think of everything you will need to do to accomplish this goal. Write each item on a separate 3x5 card. For writing a book, your list might include the following: write it, choose a title, choose a topic, get it printed, get it published, type it, have it proofread, have it typeset, get pictures, make an outline, research. List as many different aspects of the job as you can.

Part II—Time spent on the next step will vary, depending on the amount of time you have available. Fifteen minutes is a good length. You don't want to give students quite enough time to finish. You should encourage them to continue working on this assignment outside of class until all of the tasks can be accomplished in one hour or less. In this step, students will need some space (on the floor, a large table, a desk). Students will categorize their tasks and break down any that will take longer than one hour. They will need to make more cards to fill in the gaps. Have them lay their cards out in the shape of a pyramid and label them before picking them up. One way of labeling is to number the cards in outline form. For example, if a student has three major categories such as "Research," "Writing," and "Publishing," those cards would be labeled I, II, and III. The categories under "Research" would be labeled "IA," "IB," "IC,"

    Copyright © Houghton Mifflin Company. All rights reserved.

and so on, and cards for subcategories under the "IA" heading, for example, would be labeled "IA1," "IA2," and so forth. This labeling system will enable students to return to the task later and resume where they left off.

Planning Grid

This grid was developed by Skip Downing at Baltimore City Community College as a tool to plan each class session using an involving course model.

The sample grid provided below outlines one possible way of covering material from Chapter Six: Tests.

PLANNING GRID	
Content & Objectives Test Taking 1. **Before test:** *Study groups* *Review notes* *Predict ?'s* *Flash cards* *Postage stamp* 2. **During test:** *Do easy ?'s first* *Quiz strategies* 3. **After test:** *Understand errors* *Study incorrect answers*	1. **Preview & Review** *Importance of developing test-taking strategies:* *1. Strategies before the test* *2. Strategies during the test* *3. Strategies after the test*
	2. **Lecture (20%)** *Study groups: Rules to make them effective:* *1. Regular meeting times* *2. Bring 10 questions on 3x5 cards* *3. No socializing until all ?'s answered*
	3. **Guest Speaker (20%)** *College Survival videotape*
	4. **Exercise (20%)** *"Pop Quiz"*
	5. **Conversation (20%)** *Discuss "Impossible Quiz"* *Discuss College Survival videotape* *Best idea exchange*
	6. **Assignments** *Read Master Student article in Chapter Six*
	7. **Quiz & Evaluation** *Quiz with three-part forms*

First Day Activities

Listed here are suggestions for warm-up activities that you can use on the first day of class. Many of these are simple icebreakers to help you and your students acclimate to the classroom and the course objectives. Others are designed to help students begin work on the text itself. Also included here are tips that you might want to consider if you will be teaching a large group. As with other suggestions throughout this Course Manual, these are suggestions only. Refer to the HMClassPrep CD-ROM for a more complete listing of activities for your first day. Each chapter will have a few warm-up activities to introduce the chapter focus.

Copyright © Houghton Mifflin Company. All rights reserved.

Introducing the Text

Contributed by Lee Jones, University of Mississippi, University, MS

On the first day of class, Lee introduces his students to the text *Becoming a Master Student*. He instructs them to go through pages one through five and count the number of times that they find the word *action* or some derivative. When they have written down a number, they can go through pages six through nine looking for the number of times that the word *truth* or *truthfulness* is used. The only other direction is that they should do this as quickly as possible.

Lee points out that repetition is one of the most effective ways to learn and that once a concept is stored in memory, it is available for use at any time. He asks students to consider the particular words they were searching for in the beginning of the book. He stresses the importance of action in their lives in general and in their education in particular. He emphasizes that they will get the most from their education if they participate actively in the classroom. Lee also reminds students that truthfulness and integrity are vital components of success that they can practice consciously throughout their college careers.

This exercise introduces students to essential concepts in the college survival course. It is also a good way to familiarize students with the text and literally get them to be in touch with the pages.

"Name Tag" Exercise

The purpose of this exercise is to assist students in getting to know each other. They might also learn something about themselves.

Procedures—Distribute stick pins and 5x7 cards, and give the following instructions (draw an example card on the board as the students fill out their cards):

1. Write your name—first, middle initial, and last—in the middle of the card.
2. In the upper-left corner, write three things you are good at.
3. In the upper-right corner, name a place you would like to visit.
4. In the lower-left corner, write three things you want to achieve in college.
5. In the lower-right corner, list two things you like to do.

Variations on this exercise are endless. For example, you could list two things you are proud of, two favorite foods, the most influential person in your life, a material possession you would like to own, three words you would use to describe yourself, three qualities you look for in a friend, a peak experience in your life, and so on.

6. Pin the card to your shirt, blouse, or jacket.
7. Stand up and for the next few minutes (three to eight minutes, depending on the number of people in the class) walk around the room looking at as many cards as possible. Don't forget to look at people's faces before and after you read their cards. You must do this without talking. This is the hardest part of this exercise and potentially the most educational. Notice how you want to talk. (You will probably have to remind students to stay silent.)
8. Now get into groups of three, again without talking and preferably with people you do not know. When you are in a group of three, sit down anywhere.
9. When everyone is seated in a group, have the members of each group agree on which person is A, which is B, and which is C.
10. The A's will begin. For one minute, A will tell B and C something about himself and what he has written on his card. This doesn't have to be something extremely personal, just whatever he feels comfortable relating.
11. A's minute is up. Now, it is B's turn to do the same.
12. And now C will tell the group something about himself.
13. Before you return to your seats, cover your name tags and tell the other people in your group their names. If you have forgotten someone's name, guess.

   Copyright © Houghton Mifflin Company. All rights reserved.

Closure—When students have returned to their seats, ask each student to write a Discovery Statement on his name tag and turn it in to you. The Discovery Statements will be about students' reactions to the exercise and what they learned as a result of participating. The name tags can be your means of taking attendance for the class, and you will also have an opportunity to learn something about each student in your classroom.

Alternative—Distribute the 5x7 cards, and skip the stickpins. Have the students fill out the cards in the same way, then have them pair up and choose to be either A's or B's. First, have the A's explain their cards for one minute; then have the B's do the same. Then go around the class and ask students to introduce, by name, the student with whom they were paired. Have them tell the class something about that student.

Important—At the end of all exercises during which students meet each other, have them repeat the names of the others in their group before returning to their seats. The more people a student knows, the more comfortable he becomes.

College Survival Kit: A Creative Thinking Exercise

This exercise has been adapted from *The Creative Training Techniques Newsletter* (Minneapolis, MN) by Shirley Wileman Conrad, Ogalala Lakota College, Kyle, SD. This exercise is useful as a way to introduce the course and to demonstrate collaborative learning and creative and critical thinking.

First, put students into small "home" groups. Give each group a bag of items (eraser, rubber band, mint, etc.), with each bag having the same contents. Each group member reaches in and selects an item. Then, the groups split up, and students find others who are holding the same item. Instruct the new groups to brainstorm and generate a list of how the item represents being successful in college. You can give an example or two to help students get started. After everyone has had a chance to speak in these groups, students go back to their home groups to share their discoveries. This is also a good springboard for discussion with the class as a whole about discovering what items had particular significance for students and what was surprising to them.

The College Survival Kit

Mint—to remind us that we're worth a mint and that we can significantly contribute to the world around us

Eraser—to remind us that mistakes are unavoidable and that we have the opportunity to erase a mistake by learning from it

Marker—to remind us to make our mark as leaders and to create colorful, meaningful encounters

Circle—to remind us that we are all connected in the circle of life and that the choices we make travel around

Magnifying glass—to remind us to look closely at the choices that lie before us and to choose wisely

Rubber band—to remind us that we won't hurt ourselves if we stretch a little and that we need to know where our breaking point is

Compass—to remind us that there is always help to get us back on track

Map—to remind us that a well-laid plan will help us get to where we want to go

Rainbow ribbon—to remind us that we do not have to do this alone. There are others who are there to help us along the road.

Clown nose—to remind us that laughter is the best medicine and can see us through a myriad of situations

Mirror—to remind us that every job is a self-portrait of the person who did it

Gold medal—to remind us that attending school is like preparing for the Olympics. It takes practice, diligence, a good coach, self-motivation, and a clear picture of the goal to get the gold.

Copyright © Houghton Mifflin Company. All rights reserved.

Mastering New Stuff

Trying new techniques, changing habits, and practicing new behaviors can be uncomfortable at first. However, these activities make up much of what a college survival course is about. When describing the benefits of a course, it is wise to be honest about the challenges as well as confident in students' abilities to be successful. Here are some techniques for making this point.

Ask students to write their names with their nondominant hands, to introduce themselves to one another and to shake hands with their left hands, or to cross their arms in the opposite way from what they normally do. With practice, any of these uncomfortable activities will begin to feel natural.

Co-creating a Syllabus

To give students an opportunity to take responsibility for what they will learn in the course, involve them in creating the syllabus.

Step 1—Ask students to complete the Discovery Wheel.

Step 2—Distribute an outline of what you are planning to cover during the term. Ask students to compare the outline with the table of contents in the book, keeping in mind the discoveries they made while completing the Discovery Wheel.

Step 3—Ask students to tell you what they would suggest adding to, deleting from, or changing in your outline. Also ask them to prioritize the material and tell you what they feel is absolutely essential to cover.

Step 4—Make any changes in your outline that you feel are appropriate, and inform students about them.

Who Do You Think I Am?

This exercise is about our pictures of other people. While it is geared toward the students' pictures of you, the questions could be rewritten to get perceptions of anyone.

Generally, when we meet someone, we make up a story about who this person is based on how he looks, acts, talks, and so on. Our stories, formed very quickly, are built on assumptions, and any resemblance to reality is strictly coincidental. To demonstrate this, distribute an anonymous questionnaire early in the term with questions about yourself such as these:

What is my age?

Where was I born? Where did I grow up?

Am I married? Do I have children? How many?

What kind of car do I drive?

Would I get along with your friends? Why or why not?

Would you get along with my friends? Why or why not?

Will I be strict in grading you? Why or why not?

Do I support or oppose equal pay for equal work?

Did I vote in the last national election? For whom did I vote for president?

Am I a religious person?

What kinds of activities do I enjoy? Circle all that you think apply.

scuba diving	water-skiing	golf	cleaning house
baking	writing	tennis	reading
downhill skiing	basketball	sewing	travel

Summarize and report the results to the class and share the truth. Be prepared for a few laughs when you compare the students' pictures of you with your own pictures of yourself.

   Copyright © Houghton Mifflin Company. All rights reserved.

Tips for Teaching Large Groups

Learning Names

- Use name tags.
- Promise to learn students' names—demonstrates memory techniques as well as the effectiveness of making a promise.
- Use name tents.
- Take photos and place them on oversized cards with pertinent information. (One way to do this is by collecting student ID cards and copying them.)
- Request that students always state their names first before asking or answering a question or making a comment.
- Create a seating chart before the first class.
- If you miss a student's name in class, take that student out for coffee.
- Be willing to look foolish.

Bringing a Sense of Community to Your Classroom

- Remember students' comments and refer back to them by making references to the students' names.
- Assign students small group roles—leader, recorder, timekeeper, reporter, logistics specialist, or social director.
- Ask students to come in for individual 15-minute appointments during the first or second week of class.
- Set ground rules and consistently enforce them.

Participation in Large Classes

- Practice enthusiasm.
- Plan participation activities.
- Call on students rather than waiting for them to volunteer.
- Use a question box.
- Get students to participate:
  - Write first.
  - Share in small groups (two to four students).
  - Read anonymously submitted Discovery and Intention Statements.
- Plan variety:
  - Use a seven-part course structure.
  - Lecture less.

Handling Paperwork

- Use a travel folder—each student should have one with in/out files.
- Color-code chapters and file folders for students.
- Lay out papers alphabetically and then have students pick their own papers.
- Use a logistics person in small groups to pick up and deliver the group's papers.
- Use three-part quiz sheets so you don't have to hand back or correct quizzes.
- Use campus mail to return papers.
- Pick up and hand out papers according to seating charts.
- Have students pick up handouts before class.

Copyright © Houghton Mifflin Company. All rights reserved.

Logistics

- Use a microphone whenever possible.
- Claim the territory:
  - Wander around.
  - Be willing to be larger than life, even theatrical at times.
  - Think big about gestures and movements.
- Use student assistants to help teach content, reinforce ideas, or grade papers.
- Videotape guest speakers.
- Vary your voice level (even speaking softly at times).

Taking Attendance

- Use leftover name tags from previous classes.
- Have students sign in.
- Use quizzes, Discovery and Intention Statements, or assignments turned in as a means of taking attendance.

Resources

Bibliography

The following books are excellent sources for exercises. If you wish to try a different exercise or want to expand on what is included in this manual or the HMClassPrep CD-ROM, these books contain hundreds of ideas.

Berk, Ron. *Professors Are from Mars, Students Are from Snickers.* Madison, WI: Magna Publications, 1998. (How to deliver humor in the classroom and in professional presentations)

Canfield, J., and Harold C. Wells. *100 Ways to Enhance Self-Concept in the Classroom.* Englewood Cliffs, NJ: Prentice-Hall, 1976.

Erickson, Bette L., and Diane Strommer. *Teaching College Freshmen.* San Francisco: Jossey-Bass, 1991.

Hendricks, C. G., and R. Willis. *The Centering Book: Awareness Activities for Children, Parents and Teachers.* Englewood Cliffs, NJ: Prentice-Hall, 1975.

Hoeksema, Thomas, and Robert Holkebeor. *A Casebook for Student Leaders.* Boston: Houghton Mifflin, 1998.

Johnson, D. *Reaching Out: Interpersonal Effectiveness and Self-Actualization.* Englewood Cliffs, NJ: Prentice-Hall, 1972.

McKeachie, Wilbert J. *Teaching Tips.* Boston: Houghton Mifflin, 1999.

Pfifer, J. W., and J. E. Jones. *A Handbook of Structured Experiences for Human Relations Training. Vols. 1–10.* San Diego: University Associates, 1981.

Rydberg, D. *Building Community in Youth Groups.* Loveland, CO: Group Books, 1985.

Simon, S., L. Howe, and H. Kirschenbaum. *Values Clarification: A Handbook of Practical Strategies for Teachers and Students.* New York: Hart Publishing, 1972.

Smith, M. *A Practical Guide to Values Clarification.* La Jolla, CA: University Associates, 1977.

Von Oech, R. *A Whack on the Side of the Head.* New York: Warner Books, 1983.

Von Oech, R. *A Kick in the Seat of the Pants.* New York: HarperPerennial, 1986.

Weinstein, M. *Play Fair: Everybody's Guide to Non-Competitive Play.* San Luis Obispo, CA: Impact Publishers, 1980.

Copyright © Houghton Mifflin Company. All rights reserved.

Trainings

Many colleges want additional training for their teachers in developing lesson plans and assisting students in using this information to their benefit. You can hire trainers from the following organizations to come to your college to conduct on-site trainings. They have all contributed to the material in *Becoming a Master Student*.

College Survival, Houghton Mifflin Co., 2075 Foxfield Drive, Suite 100, St. Charles, IL 60174, 800-528-8323.

McBer & Co., 116 Huntington Avenue, Boston, MA 02116, 800-729-8074.

Web Sites

For exercises and student discussion groups online, http://collegesurvival.college.hmco.com/instructors

The New World of Work, http://www.cod.edu/facdev/leader/new.htm. Quantum Leadership Academy web site, College of DuPage, Wheaton, IL

Planning a College Course, http://www.unl.edu/teaching/PlanningCourse.html

Study Skill Checklist, http://www.ucc.vt.edu/stdysk/checklis.html

PART III:
TECHNOLOGY IN THE CLASSROOM
Ideas for First-Time Users of Technology

Dramatic increases in the use of instructional technology call for thinking about how technology affects the classroom and how it is pedagogically valuable to students and instructors. In technology-based or enhanced teaching and learning environments, it might be valuable to go back to the basics of course design. The primary aim of education, according to John Dewey, is "the development of reflective, creative, and responsible thought." According to educator John Henry Newman, the fundamental process of education is that of communication.

New modes of distance education are based on interaction. This technology promotes new forms of active participation among faculty and students, students with other students, and students with multimedia resources. This interaction need not take place in the classroom. Instead, it can take place anywhere that a computer can be hooked up to the Internet. Learning in a "virtual" classroom can provide students with opportunities to control learning at their own pace and on their own time and can also accommodate individual learning styles. The goal is to use technology in a way that enhances learning.

Following are some ways that instructors can use technology to enhance learning:

- Provide an electronic syllabus to each student via email or on the Web that can supply further information about assignments, expanding upon a printed version that is distributed in class.
- Electronically distribute lecture outlines, exam review questions, or study tips.
- Ask students to share their papers with the whole class via email, listserv, or the Web.
- Assign students to respond to questions about a case study before the class discussion.
- Provide web links on the latest data that you are currently covering in class.
- Designate one of your office hours as a "virtual" office hour during which you engage the ideas and questions sent to you by students via email. This might encourage students who don't feel comfortable speaking in class or coming to your office to talk to you.
- Encourage students to participate in the discussions on the College Survival web site.
- Ask students to complete Discovery and Intention Statements or exercises such as the Discovery Wheel on the College Survival web site.

Using the College Survival Web Site
and Other Sites

The College Survival web site can be accessed at **http://collegesurvival.college.hmco.com**. Our site is divided into separate sections for students (**http://collegesurvival.college.hmco.com/students**) and for instructors (**http://collegesurvival.college.hmco.com/instructors**). On the student portion of our site, you and your students can use our updated interactive exercises, including the online Discovery Wheel, Interactive time chart, and Create a lifeline. Check out our new exercises covering topics such as procrastination, money management, and sexual harassment. Encourage your students to participate in online discussion groups, take practice ACE quizzes to test their knowledge on chapter content, and read more about our master student profiles. Updates will be made to the web site regularly, so be sure to check

Copyright © Houghton Mifflin Company. All rights reserved.

back for other new features. Links that appear in the printed textbook will be updated here as necessary and can be found under "Internet Resources."

Instructors can access additional support materials (**http://collegesurvival.college.hmco.com/ instructors**), learn about supplements to the main text, and exchange ideas with other professors. Read back issues of our newsletter or submit an idea for a future article. Download our updated PowerPoint slides or exercises to accompany our videotapes.

If the technology is available in your classroom, provide your students with a walk-through of the College Survival web site on the first day of class. Show them how to access the Houghton Mifflin College Survival home page (**http://collegesurvival.college.hmco.com**), select "students"; choose Ellis, *Becoming a Master Student*, Tenth Edition; and click on "go." Ask them to bookmark this page or to save it in their "Favorites" folder.

When the Internet is discussed in class, it is important to remind your students to think critically about the information posted on a web site. Anyone can post information on the Web. Have your students ask themselves questions about the source of the information, how respectable and reliable the source is, and what evidence there is to support the information being presented. Also teach your students how to cite the web site as a source. Works appearing on the Web should be cited exactly like any other print material. Add the electronic address (URL) of the source at the end of the entry. For example:

> "Documenting Sources from the World Wide Web." Modern Language Association Online. 29 June 1999 <http://www.mla.org/set_stl.htm>

Visit the MLA web site (**http://www.mla.org**) for the most up-to-date information on documenting sources.

The College Survival web site also provides you with a place to meet and talk to other instructors dedicated to college survival. Join the online discussion groups and post your own ideas on different aspects of the text. Post a question and check back to see how other schools handle similar situations.

Your students can also participate in online discussion groups. Ask them to post a question during the course of the semester and also ask them to suggest an answer to a question another student has posted.

Inviting Students to Use the Web

- Ask students to visit at least one of the sites listed as an Internet resource at the end of each chapter of *Becoming a Master Student*. Invite the students to go to the Internet Resources page on the College Survival web site and submit the URLs of the sites they have found most helpful, with a brief description of what they liked best about the site.
- Ask students to find a web site that pertains to something that interests them in the text's table of contents on the first day of class. Invite them to submit their findings to be posted on the College Survival web site.
- Ask students to visit the Web to discover more information about the master students profiled in the text or to search out information about their own personal heroes.
- Ask students to visit your school's home page and conduct a scavenger hunt for resources available to them. The kinds of information that the students can search for include library hours, computer resources, academic advising, public safety tips, financial aid, professional organizations, and specific degree requirements.
- Assign students to teams of three to search the Web for additional information on material from a chapter of *Becoming a Master Student*.
- Invite students to investigate the Web for unique career opportunities.
- Have students access one of the online Learning Style Inventories (LSIs) described in the text and then take the test.

Copyright © Houghton Mifflin Company. All rights reserved.

Using Your HMClassPrep CD-ROM

The goal of the HMClassPrep CD-ROM that accompanies *Becoming a Master Student* is to provide you with instructional resources that you can use in electronic form. Each resource is provided in the file format we think will be most useful to you: Microsoft Word files for documents you might want to edit, PowerPoint files for presentation, and a videotape to help you use the Learning Styles Inventory in your course. Most resources can be customized to match exactly the way you teach your class.

You can access the files on HMClassPrep directly through the HMClassPrep interface. This interface organizes resources for you by chapter or by asset type. Using the HMClassPrep interface, you can open files in their appropriate applications, use them as they are, or modify them and save them to your hard drive.

If you wish to access files without using the HMClassPrep interface, you can find all of the resources in this application in a folder titled Assets on the root level of your CD. The Word file contents.doc, also on the root level of your CD, provides a list of all HMClassPrep files and their file names.

HMClassPrep for Dave Ellis, *Becoming a Master Student*

HMClassPrep for Dave Ellis, *Becoming a Master Student* gathers in one place a variety of resources to make your college survival course easier to teach. Within an easy-to-navigate interface, HMClassPrep gives you the following assets created specifically for *Becoming a Master Student*:

- An introduction to the CD-ROM for the instructor
- A transition guide for moving from the previous edition of the book
- Sample syllabi
- Descriptions of all components available for the college survival course
- Exercises for each chapter in *Becoming a Master Student*
- Lecture ideas for each chapter in *Becoming a Master Student*
- A customizable test for each chapter in *Becoming a Master Student*
- A PowerPoint slide presentation for each chapter in *Becoming a Master Student*
- An overview of the Learning Styles Inventory
- A videotape—*The Learning Styles Inventory: A Tool for Teacher and Student Success*
- An index to the contents of the CD-ROM

Help and a web link to additional textbook resources are both accessible via buttons on the HMClassPrep interface.

Using HMClassPrep

To begin using HMClassPrep, click the textbook image on the title screen. You will then be on the main screen of HMClassPrep, from which you can access all chapter materials and assets. How you access the files in HMClassPrep will depend to some degree on your browser and operating system. For specific information pertaining to your system and browser, click the Help button in the green navigation bar.

To access chapter materials and assets, click a chapter number and title in the left menu, and the chapter's assets will appear on the right. Then, click an asset to launch the asset in its application, such as Microsoft Word or PowerPoint. You can now print documents, save them to your hard drive, cut and paste material from them, or edit them. After you edit documents, be sure to save them to your hard drive. (Note: Office files will be marked "Read-Only." These files can be edited. Save them to your hard drive using the Save As command on the File menu and name them accordingly.)

Viewing PowerPoint Presentations

If you have the PowerPoint application (not the Viewer) installed and launch a PowerPoint presentation from within the HMClassPrep interface, you might need to then play the presentation. You can do this in one of the following ways:

- Click the Slide Show icon in the lower-left corner of the presentation window.
- On the Slide Show menu, click View Show.
- On the View menu, click Slide Show.

    Copyright © Houghton Mifflin Company. All rights reserved.

You must have the full PowerPoint application to edit and save the PowerPoint slides included on HMClassPrep. If you do not have the full PowerPoint application, you must install the PowerPoint Viewer to play the slide presentations.

Windows users can install the PowerPoint Viewer (ppview97.exe for Windows) directly from the Plug-ins folder on your CD-ROM. Using Windows Explorer or My Computer, locate the root level directory of the HMClassPrep CD, and double-click the file ppview97.exe to open the installer. You will be guided through the installation process.

Macintosh users, to install the PowerPoint Viewer, must drag the folder Microsoft PowerPoint 98 Viewer to their hard drive. This folder is in the Plug-ins folder on your CD-ROM.

Launching PowerPoint from Internet Explorer with Windows 2000 or NT

If you are using Internet Explorer with Windows 2000 or NT 4.0, your PowerPoint slide presentation, when launched from HMClassPrep, will open in Slide Show mode. To edit the slide presentation, click the browser's Edit menu, and then click Edit slides. To display PowerPoint toolbars, from the View menu, choose Toolbars and then select the toolbars you want visible.

Customizing PowerPoint Presentations

To customize the HMClassPrep PowerPoint presentations, you must have the full version of the PowerPoint application installed on your computer. If you do not have the full version of PowerPoint installed, you can still play the presentations with the PowerPoint Viewer. Presentations played with the PowerPoint Viewer cannot be edited.

Use the following steps to customize the HMClassPrep PowerPoint presentations:

1. Create a directory on your hard drive for the PowerPoint slides. You can do this in Windows Explorer or My Computer. If you are a Macintosh user, create a new folder on your hard drive.
2. Open a PowerPoint presentation from HMClassPrep.
3. From within PowerPoint, on the File menu, choose Save As.
4. Choose the directory/folder you have created in which you're going to save the slides, and click Save.
5. When you have finished customizing your PowerPoint presentation, save the file as a presentation on your hard drive.

Error Message When Launching PowerPoint Presentations

Depending on your version of PowerPoint, you might get an error message when launching PowerPoint files that says that the file has Asian characters that might not display properly. This message is an indication that your version of PowerPoint is more recent than the version of PowerPoint that was used to create the files. Click OK. Your slide presentation will display properly and accurately.

Exiting HMClassPrep

To exit HMClassPrep, close your browser window and remove the CD from the CD-ROM drive.

Notes for Macintosh Users

For Macintosh users using OS X: At the time of HMClassPrep's release, final browser and Office software was not available for OS X. We encourage users of OS X to work in classic mode in OS X until native applications are available.

When launching some Electronic Solutions files, you might receive an error message that some data was lost and the file is being marked "Read-Only." Click OK. The files are usable; to edit, use the Save As command on the File menu. You might need to adjust row height to see fully the contents of the cells.

Users of Internet Explorer might notice that the fonts in some Electronic Solutions files are too large for the cells. Select all text (Command-A) and choose a smaller font size to read the worksheet.

Users of Netscape Communicator 6.1 might not be able to launch Excel files or videos. To solve, switch to Internet Explorer or a lower version of Netscape.

Troubleshooting

For detailed troubleshooting, please see Help within HMClassPrep.

Technical Support

For technical support, call Houghton Mifflin Software Support at 800-732-3223 between 9 a.m. and 5 p.m. EST, Monday through Friday, or send an email to support@hmco.com.

Course Management Systems

Course management systems are tools educators can use to deliver instructional materials, communicate with students, and take care of record keeping, scheduling, and other instructional management tasks on computer (generally using a web browser). These systems can be used to create complete, stand-alone distance education courses or to provide supplements to traditional classroom instruction. There are two types of course management systems:

- Unique systems created by individual institutions or instructors using authoring software
- Customizable preprogrammed systems offered by commercial companies on their web sites

Unique Systems

"Authoring" refers to the act of creating web sites. With authoring software, instructors can craft unique web sites that provide students with a syllabus, multimedia course materials, links to other relevant web sites, practice quizzes, exams, and more—all without knowing computer programming. Such web sites can also include "protected" pages, accessible only by the instructor, with management features that allow the instructor to track student performance, trace students' use of site components, maintain records, and so on.

There are a number of authoring programs designed specifically for educational use, ranging from full-featured, high-priced systems such as Macromedia's Authorware to simpler, cheaper dedicated programs like EasyProf and Java plug-ins for general HTML editors, such as the Course Builder extension for Macromedia's Dreamweaver program.

Authoring software gives instructors greater control than preprogrammed systems over the content and structure of their online courses. However, a commensurate amount of effort is required to learn the program, plan and construct the course elements and management features, publish the web site to a server, and maintain the server. If you are interested in publishing your own unique course web sites and if your institution offers support for one or more authoring programs, you might find these tools extremely useful. Otherwise, you might prefer the convenience and ease of use of a preprogrammed commercial course management system.

Preprogrammed Systems

Instructors can choose from a variety of ready-made commercial course management systems available on the World Wide Web. Probably the two best-known such systems are WebCT and Blackboard.com. These systems provide ready-made course structures, content, and management tools designed to be applicable to a variety of courses and subjects. Instructors create accounts for themselves on these sites and then modify preset templates to suit their own particular needs. Students enter a user name and password on the site to access course materials and schedules and to communicate with other students and the instructor. Management tools such as student performance tracking and syllabus builders are available for instructors, and sometimes ready-made, subject-specific content that instructors can modify to suit their needs is also available.

Some systems, including WebCT, encourage entire institutions to subscribe to their service, providing course templates designed specifically for the institution to provide a uniform look and feel for all of its online courses.

 Copyright © Houghton Mifflin Company. All rights reserved.

Characteristics of a Well-Designed System

A well-designed course web site includes easy, intuitive navigation between pages. Students should be able to find the information they need quickly, without becoming lost in a hyperlink jungle. They should be able to go back and review, or leave off and return to a particular point in the course, with just one or two clicks. A course web site that makes students repeatedly hit the "back" arrow on their browser to review, or start over at the beginning if they take a break, is not well designed.

A course web site should offer flexibility as well, particularly if it is to be used for a pure distance learning course. It should put the student in control, allowing her the option of choosing how to progress through the course materials.

Good web courses are interactive, prompting students to input information through practice quizzes or other features, and providing feedback on their responses. A web course consisting of little more than onscreen reading does not take advantage of the rich educational potential that the medium offers.

A course web site should take full advantage of the online environment by providing links to other relevant web sites and Internet research tools. Likewise, it should integrate Internet technologies such as IRC and email to facilitate communication among students and between students and instructors. (See the following article on distance education.) Instructors should make intelligent use of multimedia features on course web sites, remembering that not all students have broadband Internet connections. Including excessively large files on course web pages might provoke intense frustration among students with slower, dial-up connections.

Finally, a well-designed course management system is easy for the instructor to use and maintain and features instructional management tools that add genuine value. When evaluating different course management systems, don't assume that the system with the most bells and whistles is necessarily the most useful, and be aware of the potential learning curve involved with each one.

For a list of educational authoring software and commercial course management systems, see http://www.sfu.ca/person/lower/cai_articles/WebCAI.html.

Distance Education

"Distance education" refers to instruction in which students and teachers participate "at a distance," without meeting in person. Distance education is used at all educational levels, from grade schools to universities to continuing education, as well as for corporate training. Historically, distance education consisted of correspondence courses administered by mail and real time telecasts of traditional college lectures. Today, most distance education is delivered by computer, either on CD-ROM or over the Internet, in courses designed specifically for that medium.

Models of Distance Education

The Institute for Distance Education describes three models of distance education (http://www.umuc.edu/ide/modldata.html#desc-a). In the "distributed classroom" model, technology is used to extend a traditional classroom-based course to a number of off-site students. In "independent learning," students progress through course materials on their own and maintain contact with the instructor individually (usually via email). In an "open learning course," students study independently and also use telecommunications technology to attend virtual class meetings of all enrolled students.

Distance Education Technologies

Distance education uses technology in two ways: to transmit educational materials and to facilitate communication between people who are not physically in the same place. Instruction can be delivered synchronously, with students and instructors participating simultaneously in real time (the open learning model), or asynchronously, with students participating individually according to their own schedules (the independent learning model). Some distance education courses include both synchronous and asynchronous components.

Copyright © Houghton Mifflin Company. All rights reserved.

Computer technologies used for synchronous delivery include IRC, MOOs, and MUDs. Technologies used for asynchronous delivery include email, listservs, and web sites.

Internet relay chat (IRC)—IRC is the Internet equivalent of an old-fashioned party line telephone connection. IRC software allows users at different locations to chat in real time via typed messages. Participants log on to a server (by telnet or via a web page) and select the appropriate conversation, or channel. When a user enters a message on her computer, the message is immediately displayed to all of the other users logged on to that particular channel. IRC can connect hundreds of users at a time, and users can drop in on a conversation at any time. IRC conversations can be recorded in logs for future reference.

MUDs and MOOs—While these are similar to IRC, instead of a party line they are more like virtual rooms in which people can meet, converse, and even examine and exchange virtual objects. Multi-user dungeons (MUDs) predate the World Wide Web. They were originally developed for the game *Dungeons and Dragons* ("dungeons" are now more often called "domains") and are generally structured around some sort of theme, such as a famous building or a historical period. Thus, they are particularly effective for education. Students can tour virtual worlds (such as the Land of Oz or T. S. Eliot's Wasteland), meet historical figures, and conduct collaborative experiments with "lab" partners located around the globe. MOOs are object-oriented MUDs that allow the user to place objects in the virtual space for others to examine or manipulate and to upload programs that will execute commands even after the user logs off.

Email and listservs—Electronic mail, or email, is the most popular Internet application for both educational and general use. Instructors can inform students of assignments and schedules by email and transmit educational materials to students as email attachments. Students can submit completed assignments to instructors via email as well. List servers, or listservs, are email servers programmed to manage electronic mailing lists. An instructor can set up a mailing list for a course on a campus listserv, and students can subscribe to it to receive course notices and send messages to all of the other list members. At a set interval (usually once a day), the listserv will send an email to all of the list subscribers, containing every message posted to the list during that period. This can be done automatically, or the instructor can screen the messages before they are sent to the list subscribers.

Web sites—A web site can provide an entire, self-contained course. Students can access multimedia course materials, links to web-based research materials, class notices and syllabi, practice quizzes and exams, and more. Instructors can create schedules, post notices, and track student performance. Student responses to practice quizzes and exams are delivered to instructors automatically by email. Although web sites are used primarily for asynchronous delivery, they can incorporate technologies such as live chat that are used for synchronous communication as well. For more information on educational applications of web sites, see the articles on course management systems and web resources in this Part.

Advantages and Drawbacks

The main advantages to distance education are flexibility and convenience. Students do not need to travel to a remote location and can learn from the comfort of their own home or office. In the case of asynchronous distance education, students do not need to follow a set schedule. They can complete their work whenever they choose, at their own pace. In addition, well-designed web-based courses make full use of the information riches that the Internet offers, placing supporting information just a click away.

A potential downside to distance learning is the lack of personal interaction between students and instructors. For some people, learning is easier in a social setting, where they can ask questions and take cues from the instructor's voice and body language. This problem can be mitigated, however, through the use of interactive technologies such as IRC, and even through regular email. For some students, the anonymity of electronic communication is actually preferable to participating in a classroom setting, with other students listening and watching.

For more information on distance education, see the Distance Education Clearinghouse web site at **http://www.uwex.edu/disted/home.html**, a portal site with numerous links to distance education resources on the Web.

 Copyright © Houghton Mifflin Company. All rights reserved.

Online Becoming a Master Student

Maximizing the interactive web environment to promote active learning, reflective writing, and immediate application of skills and processes, *Online Becoming a Master Student* can be used as a stand-alone, customized Internet course or as a web-based component, perfect for incorporating more technology in the classroom. Content from the text is not replicated online. Additional readings, assignments, interactive activities, discussion groups, quizzes, and tests are available for each chapter of *Becoming a Master Student*.

The online course is available on two platforms—Blackboard and WebCT—and has been updated to accompany the Tenth Edition. The textbook, required reading for the online course, is shrink-wrapped with an e-token, providing students with access to your customized course, for an additional $14 (net) plus the price of the textbook.

A Facilitator's Guide and instructions for uploading the course content are available on the College Survival web site (**http://collegesurvival.college.hmco.com**).

An interactive demonstration is available for instructors interested in viewing the content and structure. Contact your sales representative or College Survival consultant for details.

Creating an Online Course

Contributed by Diane Beecher, Lake Superior College, Duluth, MN

When I first decided to create an online version of my school's college survival course, it was before the development of a campus distance education committee and before its decision to use a software package that would help to build and maintain an online course. So I spent many hours setting up web pages that would explain to students what I wanted them to do and how to get the assignments and quizzes to me. Basically, the web pages ended up being a course outline with links to the assignments. They were only a rough approximation of what I really wanted. I craved an area on the Web that would be password protected and would allow students to take quizzes and do assignments online. Little did I know that such a thing was being developed by several companies. Then I found out about online delivery software.

I was next invited to join a group of pioneers who would meet during the summer months, using an authoring program to develop an online course. I was pleased to learn that the software would allow me to do everything I had envisioned and more. I was able to set up lecture notes, assignments, quizzes and tests, a bulletin board, email, a chat room, links to Internet resources, a glossary, a calendar, and a grading system.

I started out by designing a welcome page that I thought would be inviting to students. I needed it to be an advertisement to students with links to more information for those who were interested in the course. I linked the course web site to the web site I had developed for our department. Then I set up a home page with buttons that led to the various components of the course, as previously mentioned. The first button led to an explanation of every component of the online course, which students could read through before they started working through the course and could refer to if necessary at any time during the semester.

Keep in mind that your site should be easy to navigate so that students don't get lost in a myriad of seemingly disconnected web pages. The organization of the course should be obvious to students. Their job is to take the course, not to figure out what you are trying to do. The software should allow the teacher to develop a "path" for students to follow. You choose what goes into the path. In my course, students are able to access the syllabus, a course outline, and a web page for each chapter in *Becoming a Master Student*. They click on the name of the chapter we are covering that week and are able to view the pages assigned, glossary entries for key terms, lecture notes, the assignment (which they are required to post to the bulletin board), and a link to an interactive quiz.

Tips for teachers who are considering online courses
- Use software that other professors at your college are using so that it is possible to have general training sessions for all students taking online courses and so that the teachers of the courses can train each other.

Copyright © Houghton Mifflin Company. All rights reserved.

- The software should be easy to use, even by nontechnical people.
- Don't settle for a software package that has only a few features, thinking that you really don't need many. Eventually, as you develop your course, you will probably want more.
- The software program shouldn't require expert knowledge of HTML (hypertext markup language) or other markup languages.
- Your online course shouldn't require students to have any special software. They should be able to access the course through their web browsers.

It is important to include related Internet links so that students can become aware of and take advantage of the wealth of material available on the Web. Fortunately, the current editions of *Becoming a Master Student* include a list of online resources for each chapter, as well as links to pages on the Houghton Mifflin College Survival web site.

Interaction is also important to students. Cooperative skills will help them adjust to real-world situations on the job and in the community. Our department feels so strongly about fostering these skills that we have recently added the goal of learning cooperative skills to our syllabus as a course outcome. Take advantage of bulletin board and chat room features to encourage students to work cooperatively in groups. There are many exercises in *Becoming a Master Student*, this Course Manual, and the HMClassPrep CD-ROM that can be adapted for group use. For example, you can ask students to post reactions to other students' postings. Another assignment would be to have students respond to a case study regarding a problem-solving situation relating to one of the text chapters.

Unless you want your online course to be a substitute for an independent study course, you should establish a schedule with due dates for assignments and quizzes. Otherwise, it is very difficult to have students working collaboratively. A schedule also encourages students to stay up-to-date. Procrastinators might sign up for online courses and have a difficult time staying motivated enough to complete work in a timely manner. I try to stay on top of these students with regular emails, if necessary. No matter what we do, we will always have students who will not make timelines. All we can do is try our best. The rest is up to them!

When you start to develop an online course, it is a good idea to organize your thoughts before you plunge into the actual development of your course. Use a flow chart to write out your ideas first so that you can "see the forest"!

It isn't necessary to do it all during the first term (semester or quarter). Make sure that you include what you absolutely need; you can worry about the fancy stuff later. As teachers, our courses are always evolving. It's no different with an online course. It will always be a work in progress. Students are always a good resource for suggestions. Ask them what they would like to see in your online course.

As Dave Ellis says in his seven-day antiprocrastination plan, "Settle it now." If you have been thinking about putting together an online course, decide right now that you are going to do it, and then start mapping out a plan.

Mastering the College Experience:
A Telecourse for *Becoming a Master Student*

Mastering the College Experience is an integrated instructional system that combines stimulating and informative video lessons produced by the Emmy Award-winning Coast Telecourses with Houghton Mifflin's best-selling *Becoming a Master Student* text, a Telecourse Student Guide, and a Faculty Manual. The course is designed to be offered in a variety of formats, including broadcast, cablecast, or videotape delivery, under an instructor's direction. Telecourse students study independently, watching the video lessons and reading the course-related materials on their own, at home, in a learning center, at a training site, or at the workplace.

    Copyright © Houghton Mifflin Company. All rights reserved.

Mastering the College Experience has been instructionally designed to meet the needs of students who are entering college from high school or are returning to further their education. There are 26 half-hour videotapes providing examples, methods, and resources in an engaging format. Students will be introduced to key concepts as they watch students learn and discuss the process based on discovering the power of self-responsibility. *Mastering the College Experience* features real situations experienced by real students enrolled in college. The telecourse documents the adversities and accomplishments of seven students from different ethnic and socioeconomic backgrounds as they learn core study skills as well as life skills.

A Telecourse Student Guide for *Mastering the College Experience* (published by Houghton Mifflin Company) contains overviews that summarize critical information and terms in each lesson. It serves as an important bridge between the textbook, which is required reading for participating in the course, and the video components. Lesson objectives alert students to course expectations and the information that they must acquire from each lesson in order to successfully master their own college experience. A Faculty Manual (published and distributed by Coast Learning Systems) contains information on managing the course. There are program descriptions, lesson objectives, suggestions for communicating effectively with students, a checklist of tasks for the instructor, ideas for supplementary activities, suggested techniques for providing support to students, and a list of useful references and resources. A complete test bank is also included.

Creating a Telecourse

Organizing a telecourse is very different from organizing a traditional course or providing course functions online because you are using the medium of television. Television provides different kinds of teaching opportunities and places certain constraints on what you do. Another factor is distance. You will be dealing with students at different distances. How you personalize your course and how you interact with your students will influence their attitudes toward future telecourse involvement. Teaching on TV requires a team approach involving the instructor, television staff, graphics and photography staff, and instructional design and clerical staff.

Traditional courses must be modified for presentation over instructional television in order to take advantage of the strengths of the medium. This includes interaction at remote sites, a high level of visualization, and the use of handouts correlated with the television graphics. Students should spend 30 to 50 percent of their time interacting with other students in learning activities at remote sites. When teaching on instructional television, instructors should do the following:

- Think simultaneously about what is to be taught and in what sequence.
- Determine how much time should be devoted to each segment.
- Decide what will appear on the TV screen.
- Determine what activities the students are to do at field sites.
- Plan how students will identify and record important notes in some sort of study guide.

These four areas will need to be modified:
1. Instructional design
2. Television graphics
3. Student handouts
4. Telelesson plans

Before You Begin Your Lesson Plan
Consider whether you would teach the same way if the following conditions were to apply:
- You are physically separated from your students.
- You cannot see your students and have no visual feedback.
- Handouts are required rather than optional.
- Your students won't ask questions.

Copyright © Houghton Mifflin Company. All rights reserved.

- You are talking to a TV camera lens.
- A 50-minute telelecture takes exactly 50 minutes.
- Involving students at off-campus sites is critical.
- Classes can be videotaped.

As you review your telelesson plan, look for areas in which you can do the following:
- Visualize.
- Create interactivity among students at individual sites and among sites.
- Focus attention through cues and prompts.
- Utilize the best aspects of the medium.
- Motivate students to higher levels of learning.
- Use artifacts, videotapes, and handouts.

The Teacher's Role
- The key to success in distance learning is the teacher.
- Teachers must find new ways to structure student-teacher interaction.

Instructional Elements
- Meet in person with students in each of the remote class sites early in the course.
- Have telephone office hours.
- Set up assignments that students can follow as members of learning groups.

Teaching Strategies
- Visualize what you want the course to be.
- Balance content with activities.
- Develop strategies to avoid broadcasting "talking heads."
- Create legible screen text and graphics.
- Familiarize yourself with the camera and audio setup.
- Visit remote sites to meet students.

Building Interaction
- Send students a welcome letter and syllabus.
- Refer to students by their names, not by their locations.
- Instruct students on how to use the equipment.
- Involve students at all sites.
- Make sure students get to know one another at all sites.
- Allow time for students to explore the meaning of the material.
- Plan for interaction. Do not wait for it to happen by itself.
- A good rule of thumb is to aim for interaction time to make up one-quarter to one-third of the total course.
- Share information with learners about additional readings, library resources, and community resources.

First Class Session
Plan your first class session and the students' introduction to a distance education class to orient them and give them a sense of confidence in the new technology. If they've never been in a teleclassroom, students might feel self-conscious at first and might need to adjust to seeing themselves on TV.

There are four things that should occur during your first class, not necessarily in the following order:

1. An ice-breaking exercise, such as pair interviews
2. Joint agreement on protocol in a distance education classroom. Discuss class logistics, courier service, email, faxing, and your office and telephone hours. It's important for students to know what cue to

 Copyright © Houghton Mifflin Company. All rights reserved.

use to get your attention. It could be a click, a tap, or a flash card. Emphasize that it's the students' responsibility to let you know if they are having trouble seeing or hearing. You might want to repeat this information several times during the early days of the class for the sake of students who are not comfortable interrupting you to ask a question.

3. Distribution of handouts and discussion of your syllabus, timeline of class events, due dates for assignments, and exam dates
4. Basic orientation to the technology. Give a brief explanation and demonstration of the pieces of equipment that you'll be using in the class. If you plan to allow students to use the equipment themselves for presentations, you might want to say something at the outset, so that students will pay closer attention to how you make use of it.

Opening a Telelesson

Student attention is highest during the first 10 minutes and the last five minutes of a teleclass. Effective openings and closings are therefore essential. Following are some suggestions.

Grab their attention.
Create interest.
Fire their imaginations.
Arouse curiosity.
Energize.
Agitate.
Appeal to their passions.
Appeal to past experiences.
Create strong visual images.
Make humorous comparisons.
Make mental images.
Use analogies with visuals.
Create word pictures.
Compare the not-so-obvious.
Look for resemblances.

Create excitement and anticipation.
Shock them.
Create a desire for more.
Use theatrics.
Appeal to students' natural inquisitiveness.
Inspire.
Stimulate possibilities.
Appeal to dreams.
Exaggerate.
Stimulate new connections—"Why not?" "What if?"
Arouse emotions.
Electrify.
Wrap your key point in a story.
Did you know that . . . ?
Quotation of the day.

Closing a Telelesson

Summarize key points.
Create curiosity about what is to come.
Capture students' imaginations.
Grab their curiosity.

Information to Include
in a Syllabus for a Telecourse

Administrative Information

- Course name, catalog number, and section
- Meeting time and location (including labs)
- Biographical sketch of course instructor
- Instructor's office hours, address, and telephone number
- Where messages can be left
- On-site visitations, if appropriate

Copyright © Houghton Mifflin Company. All rights reserved.

- Procedures for on-campus visits by students
- Instructor's availability via telephone
- What to do in the event of instructor's unscheduled absence

General Course Information
- General course description, rationale, benefits
- Prerequisite courses and/or skills
- Course goals and objectives
- Class policies
  - Attendance on campus and at sites
  - Excused absences—definition and procedures
  - Drop/add procedures
  - Tardiness—impact on broadcast and on grade
  - Incomplete grade—conditions required for granting
  - Makeup tests
  - Interruptions during a telelecture—questions, etc.
  - Homework—if tardy, criteria for acceptance

Grading Procedures
- Tests and exams
- Class participation
- Papers and projects—assessment criteria
- Extra credit—limits
- How final grade is calculated
- Textbooks and library reading on reserve

Class Information
- Course calendar by week
- Titles of telelecture topics by date
- Correlated text and outside readings by topic
- Tests and exams—makeup dates
- Holidays
- Papers due
- Instructor's professional travel—substitute lecture or excused class

Creating a Positive Image for Interactive Television

Personal appearance requires some considerations when teaching on television. Here are some suggestions for adapting your presentation style and appearance.

Clothing and Accessories
- Avoid shiny jewelry, dangling earrings, and beeping watches that might be distracting. Pearls, gold button earrings, and small gold neck chains look good on TV.
- Avoid wearing strong plaids, houndstooth checks, or bold stripes, although simple prints or large outline prints with only a little detail are fine.
- Avoid wearing black and dark blue clothing, although lighter blue, gray, warm brown, pink, tan, cream, light purple, green, or beige colors work well. Avoid white and pale colors that are close to white because the fluorescent lighting typically used in distance classrooms washes out color.

   Copyright © Houghton Mifflin Company. All rights reserved.

- If you have a light complexion, never wear yellow or gold as it tends to make you look yellow, hits your face under the lights, and creates a camera glare that is too shiny to look at.
- Wear strong, vivid colors; red, however, tends to smear from pink to purple. Remember that if you take off your jacket, the color of your shirt or blouse will become the dominant color.
- Be aware of the impact of your skin and hair color, your outfit, and the backdrop. If you have a dark complexion, avoid dark colors. If you have a light complexion, avoid pale colors.
- Wear clothes that have clean lines and a classic look. Bulky shoulder pads and gathered sleeves look awkward.

Eyes

In a telecourse, your eyes are your most important feature. Use them to full advantage when you look directly at the camera. Raise an eyebrow, narrow your eyes to slits, open them wide, and, most important of all, smile with your eyes. As much as possible, keep your eyes steady and unblinking.

Hair

The smoother your hairstyle appears on camera, the more smoothly you will come across as a presenter to the audience. Curls, teased hair, and ribbons are not recommended. Hair piled on top of your head gives the appearance of a pointed head. Men should shave before a TV appearance to avoid a five-o'clock shadow. A beard or mustache should also be well groomed.

Hands

Keep hand movements to a minimum. Avoid putting your hands in your pockets or jingling coins and keys. Nail polish should not be worn because it causes unwanted shine and glare. Don't scratch your head, bat your eyes, pull your ears, or make any other distracting gesture.

Do use your hands to make a point or to direct viewers' attention to a particular visual for emphasis.

Plan All Movements

Visualize the camera as a real student. Look at the camera periodically, just as you would look at any student in the room. Off-site students need to have eye contact with you to maintain their attention and interest.

Body position is a strong means of communication. You have several choices. Facing the students full front is the strongest position. Three-quarters front is the next strongest position, while a profile position is the third strongest. The one-quarter position, with your back nearly turned toward the students, is the weakest position.

If you use different positions, here are some examples of transition statements you can use while moving:

- "I am going to draw this schematic on the dry marker board."
- "Let me move to the podium."
- "Let's look at a few slides."

Plan your movements ahead of time. Decide whether you will be sitting at the desk, using the dry marker board, pacing while carrying note cards, or using a combination of these techniques. Movement can be used to underscore important points. Experienced speakers often signal the beginning of a new topic by pausing and shifting position, possibly also walking to a different part of the room. Remember not to stand in front of visuals that must be seen.

On Camera

- Verify image and sound communication with each site when you begin the class, unless a technician has already done so.
- Establish an upbeat tempo right at the start. The first 90 seconds of a transmission are crucial for setting the pace for what follows. A new start occurs after each break, as well as at the beginning of class, and each start is a new beginning for you.

Copyright © Houghton Mifflin Company. All rights reserved.

- Appear cheerful, confident, and enthusiastic, even if something unexpected occurs. Your smile is important.
- Look directly into the camera so that students at remote sites can sense that you're looking directly at them. To create an even more personal presence, move closer to the camera or have it zoom in on you.
- Speak clearly, distinctly, and a little more slowly than you ordinarily speak. The microphone should pick up your voice unless you've turned away from it. Don't speak more loudly unless students indicate that you aren't being heard.
- Here's a stage tip to engage the listeners: Raise or inflect your voice at the end of your sentences, especially with questions.
- To stay in camera range, limit your standing or walking to one area of the classroom or to areas you know are covered by preset camera angles.
- Try to create a realistic expectation of technology. Technical problems might occur. When they do, the class might have to wait while the technician does troubleshooting. During such time, do what performers do: Maintain your sense of humor and wit. If you have backup activities created for just such a time, it won't be difficult to keep your students actively learning.
- Monitor your pace. If you're feeling low on energy or are losing the attention of students at your remote sites, ask for a response or introduce an interactive exercise.
- Select one student at each site to be a group leader to help hand out materials, assist with small group sessions, or operate the equipment.
- Give a balanced amount of attention to each class site. Take steps to keep remote-site students from feeling left out. Remote-site students might bond to help one another with communication and might even compete with students at other sites for your attention. Foster enjoyable inter-site competitiveness with intersite activities such as a quiz show or group presentations, which can be rated by you or the students themselves.
- Don't assume that students at a remote site who appear to be talking among themselves are being inattentive or disruptive. They might be helping one another understand a concept or might be developing group coherence as a means to communicate through the technology. However, the chatting might also be your cue to switch instructional gears or to signal a break.
- Address students by name to elicit a comment or response to a question. Use name tags or tent cards with thick, dark lettering about two inches high to help you identify students. You can also use a student roster and call on specific students for a response.
- Rather than making statements, ask questions often, especially ones that can relate the students' own daily experiences to your class material.
- Remember to repeat students' questions or pertinent comments to ensure that students at other sites hear them.
- From time to time, announce class breaks and change your presentation style to help pace inter-action and instruction. For example, you can lecture at a desk or board, schedule student group presentations, or elicit feedback.

Feedback

Put yourself in the seats of your students at the origination site and at the remote sites. Think in terms of what your audiences are seeing, hearing, and experiencing. Ask yourself questions such as: What if I were a student, and someone else were doing what I'm doing? Am I being as effective as I want to be? What other ways might I present this material for learning reinforcement or to avoid technical difficulties?

Get feedback directly from the students to assess their comprehension of what you're presenting since they, too, are a part of the learning experience and not just a passive audience.

If you plan on giving feedback, it's important that students at all sites receive papers and tests from you at the same time to avoid showing favoritism to any one site.

  Copyright © Houghton Mifflin Company. All rights reserved.

Personal Presentation Style

What you're trying to create in a teleclass is your personal presentation style, one that is comfortable and effective for you.

- You might include much discussion and very little lecturing.
- You might like to show graphics to illustrate or expand upon concepts, then break into small group discussions for reinforcement.
- You might choose to rely on videotapes and never use the wall-mounted board, or you might use the wall-mounted board in combination with the computer.

Be open to expanding your personal presentation style more than you would in the traditional classroom. If it's your first teleclass, start out with what makes you comfortable. Then, as you become more confident with the technology, you'll add more to your class.

Copyright © Houghton Mifflin Company. All rights reserved.

PART IV:
DIVERSE CLASSROOMS AND
RETENTION STRATEGIES

Diverse Classrooms

Research indicates that while successful students benefit from having a relationship with a caring and competent adult, they are most likely to be successful if they have a positive peer support group. The information here will help you foster that sense of belonging and assist students in sharing their discoveries of higher education. Teachers and students are currently using *Becoming a Master Student* in the United States, Canada, and many other countries. However, a variety of cultural and life experiences will most likely be represented by the students in your class. They will come from many places with varied experiences.

This section of the Course Manual and the additional activities in the Diversity chapter of the HMClassPrep CD-ROM will offer possible ways to encourage communication among students of different races, ethnicity, ages, countries of origin, and levels of familiarity with the American language and American customs.

One of the major goals of diversity awareness is to understand how each person fits into the lives and world of others. For some of your students, college might be their first experience with someone different from themselves. Keep in mind as you prepare for your course that some kinds of diversity can be less obvious—but just as profound—as others. To the student from rural America, a classmate from New York or Chicago might seem nearly as strange as one from Finland or Zimbabwe (and vice versa).

International students will have additional adjustment issues beyond those of the other students in your class. They are far from home in a culture that is foreign to them. Keep in mind that some statements, activities, or attitudes that seem perfectly natural in our society might seem curious or even offensive to international students. Familiarize yourself with cultural differences and issues that could baffle or frustrate your students from other countries and work to overcome them before they become obstacles to learning.

Finding common ground can be an important learning experience in the classroom. Routinely pairing students from different backgrounds and circumstances when assigning group projects and activities can provide students with the opportunity to encounter ideas, attitudes, and experiences different from their own. Throughout the semester, schedule activities or exercises that accentuate the similarities among your students and also celebrate the differences.

School Strategies

Promote participation—Involving students in school activities challenges them and stimulates their interest. Promote the benefits of participating by placing "ads" in the school newsletters and putting notes on bulletin boards. Design and display posters. Ask other teachers to announce school activities in their classrooms. Brainstorm ways to get more students involved. Don't overlook asking students!

Provide tutors—Encourage students to take advantage of tutors. Maintaining or improving one's performance level and gaining confidence in academic ability help ensure student success.

   Copyright © Houghton Mifflin Company. All rights reserved.

Structure opportunities for friendships—Having friends is widely accepted as a critical component of making a healthy adjustment to college life and achieving academic success. Friendships can be expanded beyond immediate peer groups to include faculty, staff, counselors, role models, peers from home environments, community members, or graduate students. Organize ice-breakers and get-acquainted exercises during orientation and at other school events. Encourage the use of name tags at these events. Sponsor social activities that include faculty and staff as well as students. Encourage broad participation in all social, academic, cultural, and extracurricular events.

Examine policies and procedures—Review policies and procedures, looking for any subtle (or blatant) messages of racism or other forms of discrimination. If there is not a clear disciplinary procedure for infractions of any policy, implement one.

Promote resources—New students who are unfamiliar with the resources at your school won't use them. Asking the administrators and staff who are responsible for these resources to describe their services during student orientation is only the beginning of what's possible.

Ask administrators and directors of service programs to speak in your course. Suggest that clubs and organizations offering services to diverse students sponsor programs to familiarize students with the resources at your school. Write articles about resources for the school newsletter. An open house at which refreshments are served invites students to get to know the facilities and the services that are available. Ask students who have benefited from the resources to give testimonials. Create contests and games that require students to visit various offices, facilities, and services personnel.

Promote the resources at your school in such a way that they attract and serve students. Have tutors and counselors introduce themselves and make short presentations in class. Ask the student advisory board for help.

Make school inviting—Students who feel comfortable are more likely to experience success in school. Do the residence halls offer quiet places to study? Are exercise facilities available at convenient times? Are the needs for student transportation and day care facilities met? Are computers up-to-date? How long do students wait for assistance in the financial aid and other student services offices? What is the quality of the food service? Would you eat what is served? How can registration procedures be more efficient? Do instructors post office hours and keep them? What do admissions representatives say would attract more students?

Hire from different backgrounds—Whenever possible, hiring both men and women from a variety of backgrounds will provide role models for students. Whether they are faculty, staff, or administrators, they should be knowledgeable about diversity issues and committed to being involved with students on campus.

Evaluate faculty—Conduct regular student and peer evaluations of all instructors. Include the criteria of being sensitive to the needs of all students and being able to adapt to facilitate the learning of all students.

Encourage leadership—Students from diverse backgrounds who are in leadership positions help promote acceptance and inclusion of all students in all areas of school life. Sponsor leadership training programs. Encourage students with leadership potential to consider running for student offices.

Sponsor panel discussions—Invite students from a variety of populations to participate in panel discussions on a wide range of topics. Each panel member can introduce himself (including a description of what it's like to be a member of his particular population on your campus, if appropriate) and then state his point of view about the topic. The discussion can then be opened for questions and answers.

Conduct workshops—Invite faculty and staff to attend workshops on the diverse backgrounds, circumstances, and cultural differences of students at your institution.

Copyright © Houghton Mifflin Company. All rights reserved.

Classroom Strategies

Help ensure success—You can individualize your instruction and structure your course so that students experience success. Total success in school is achieved by taking a series of small, successful steps. Set high and realistic expectations. If your course is too easy, students will lose interest. If it is too difficult, students might become discouraged. By continually evaluating students, monitoring their progress, and getting feedback from them, you can plan your classes in ways that help ensure student success.

Provide opportunities to talk—Invite students to speak about their perspectives. Suggest that students talk to others and share their concerns, celebrations, compliments, and complaints. Use small group discussions and exercises. Promote the idea of visiting with counselors and forming peer support groups. The suggestions for conversations and sharing on the HMClassPrep CD-ROM include many ideas for stimulating discussions.

Acknowledge and appreciate cultural differences—We can learn from each other and from exploring values that are different from our own. When we exchange ideas, we can expand our perceptions and examine our values.

Use conversations and sharing seeds, publications, and special events to recognize and celebrate diversity.

Communicate the advantages of being bicultural—Learning new ways of speaking and behaving does not mean denying or letting go of our traditional languages or methods of doing things. Adding alternatives does not eliminate anything. Expanding our options increases our ability to operate effectively in a variety of situations and improves our chances of success.

Discuss how the school environment is similar to, and different from, students' home environments. Then discuss ways to make effective transitions back and forth from one to the other. Explore how the expectations of one environment can be assets or liabilities in another. Recognize that a strength in one culture might be a detriment in another. Tennis rackets are great on a tennis court; they don't work very well in a game of golf. How can a student adapt so as to be successful in both environments?

Recognize different orientations to time, competition, and respect for authority—In some cultures, punctuality is a plus. In others, time is not measured in hours, minutes, and seconds; instead, it is measured by the movement of the sun, the changing of the seasons, and an intuitive sense of community readiness. In some cultures, competition is a common incentive. In others, it is considered antisocial and insulting. Eye contact during conversations is considered respectful in some cultures and disrespectful in others.

You can respect a wide range of orientations and, at the same time, communicate the expectations of your institution. An advantage to being bicultural is the ability to adopt behaviors that promote success in a specific environment.

Encourage exposure to different backgrounds—Encourage students to break out of old patterns and habits by associating with people from different backgrounds, as well as with those whose backgrounds are similar to their own. They could choose new lab partners, form groups with people they don't know for in-class exercises, sit in new areas in the student union, or attend events that are likely to draw crowds different from those with whom they are comfortable. Invite your class to brainstorm ways to gain exposure to people with different backgrounds.

Survey student needs—Evaluate frequently. When you become aware that a student is struggling in a certain area, make an appointment with that student to formulate an action plan.

Individualize feedback—Students appreciate getting specific feedback about their individual performance. Write relevant comments on papers you return. Send messages and comments to students through the school mail. Thank a student who has actively participated as he leaves the classroom.

   Copyright © Houghton Mifflin Company. All rights reserved.

Set clear expectations—Communicate expectations clearly. State them several times in several different ways. Use examples to illustrate both what is acceptable and what isn't. Invite students to ask questions in class or to contact you during your office hours if they have any questions or concerns.

Be a mediator—As an instructor of a college survival course, you can facilitate communication between students and administrators. Pass students' complaints and compliments on to the people who are most directly involved. Ask for responses from those people and report back to the students. Follow up on all communications until they are complete.

Include other cultural experiences—Use speakers, textbooks, classroom materials, activities, and media presentations that incorporate diverse cultural experiences. Ask students, colleagues, administrators, and community members for recommendations.

Use a critical thinking approach—Ask students to decide what they think about relevant issues and why they think it. Then ask them to seek other views and gather evidence to support the various views. Discuss which view or views are the most reasonable. When discussing issues, you can apply the strategies and recognize the errors in thinking that are outlined in the articles on critical thinking in the text.

Encourage proaction—When students face uncomfortable, unfamiliar, and difficult situations, they sometimes choose avoidance or give up. They might feel helpless or resentful and choose to withdraw. This is perceived as more attractive and less painful than risking embarrassment and other unpleasant feelings. Help students consider the long-term costs of giving up. Help them see the benefits of a positive, healthy, and proactive approach. Suggest a variety of alternatives for dealing with the problems they face. Suggest that rather than giving up, students can gather support and find forums to discuss and resolve their issues.

Allow personal expression—Invite students to translate material into their own words. Ask them how certain techniques, or variations of those techniques, might be applied in their own cultures.

Acknowledge student expertise—Ask students to communicate course content from their unique cultural perspective. Experiencing a concept from a different cultural perspective reinforces it. Give an assignment requiring students to combine a college survival strategy with some cultural event, personality, tradition, or value. For example, they could create original music and lyrics or describe what role a particular success strategy might have played in how a cultural hero changed history.

Use guest speakers—Invite guest speakers to your class who represent successful role models. Ask them to share struggles they have experienced and successes they have achieved. Be sure to include time for a question-and-answer period.

Personal Strategies

Avoid generalizations—All generalizations are suspect—even this one. Avoid tendencies to lump together all people of one race or culture. Consider speaking up when you hear generalizations being made.

Examine your own prejudices—If you have painful memories that contribute to your prejudices, judgments, and generalizations, examine them. Tell the truth about the costs and benefits of holding on to them. Look at how your history encouraged you to be prejudiced in certain ways. Talk about your prejudices and formulate a plan to heal and grow.

Examine your assumptions about students—Where do you imagine that your students go during their vacations? How would you expect them to spend extra money? What type of music do they enjoy? Who are their heroes? Which holidays do they celebrate? Listen for how often your assumptions direct your teaching and your conversations with students. How would your teaching and your conversations be different if you assumed nothing about students?

Copyright © Houghton Mifflin Company. All rights reserved.

Find a translator—Taking a First Step by admitting that we are unfamiliar or uncomfortable with others opens the door to bridging the gap with them. Ask around and find someone who can act as a translator between you and others. A translator is someone from the minority students' ethnic or cultural background who has successfully adapted to the majority environment. Ask others if they are willing to have this person present when you discuss various issues.

Increase your sensitivity to society's exclusions and inclusions—When we become aware of what to look for, we can see many examples of how one cultural or ethnic group excludes or includes others. Watch advertising and television shows. Listen to speeches. Examine the policies and notice the membership demographics of schools, business organizations, neighborhoods, religious institutions, athletic clubs, and social groups. Look for blatant, formal structures as well as subtle or hidden messages of exclusion and inclusion.

Reach out to students—Be sure students know your office hours. Send written invitations to each student in your class to come visit you during those hours. Talk about what students might gain if they schedule an appointment to see you or if they just drop in. Go over and talk to a student you see outside of the school environment. Write messages on papers you return about your reactions to what was written. Maintain accurate records about attendance and call students when they miss a class. Use whatever appropriate methods you can think of to let individual students know that you are personally interested in their success. Be a person with whom students can form a supportive, interpersonal relationship.

Give specific feedback—Feedback promotes college survival. Be especially sensitive to the unspoken expectations of the environment at your school and in your community. When feedback is given with a sincere desire to promote success, it is likely to be appreciated.

Racially and Ethnically Diverse Students

The Census Bureau of the U.S. government projected in 2000 that the U.S. population will increase from 281,421,986 to 404 million in 2050. By 2100 the total population will have doubled to 560 million. While these numbers are interesting, possibly daunting, by themselves, perhaps the most telling statistics concern the racial and ethnic changes that are happening now and will continue to happen. The non-Hispanic white population, for example, will drop from approximately 72 percent today to 53 percent in 2050.

Important and exciting changes are already visible in classrooms across the United States; still, many populations do not yet feel entirely comfortable in academic settings. There is much that instructors can do to change this situation, from simply being aware of it to using specific strategies in the classroom.

As the contents of this section of the Course Manual indicate, there are many diversities represented in colleges today, and it is a constant challenge for students, instructors, and institutions to meet the needs of a diverse population. In classrooms, this can be difficult because of prevalent stereotypes, lack of familiarity with others' lifestyles, and the sheer difficulty of conducting and participating in discussions about diversity.

One starting place is to understand what "ethnicity" means. Denotatively, the term "ethnic" refers to people who share a distinct race, nationality, religion, cultural heritage, or language. Connotatively, the term might be used with less precision as in the statement, "I enjoy ethnic food." An ethnicity is something that is specific, not general, and all individuals sharing an ethnicity are unique. This is why stereotypes are inappropriate, hurtful, and untrue. We can never say that everyone from a certain ethnic background is the same.

Similarly, we can never say that all members of the same race share exactly the same characteristics. Again, stereotypes are inappropriate. The term "race" might be perceived as falling under the umbrella of ethnicity; however, in its most general or vague sense, it is understood as a term describing a group of characteristics passed on by genetics. While skin color is certainly an example, this is overly simplistic. The term "race" can bring up strong emotions, and it should not be used carelessly.

  Copyright © Houghton Mifflin Company. All rights reserved.

In the best of all worlds, we would not have to think about ethnic and racial diversity. We would notice similarities rather than differences, and all people would consider themselves on exactly the same plane. This is not yet true in classrooms or other places. What can instructors do to foster a comfortable, respectful environment in their diverse classrooms? How can all students be given an equal opportunity to succeed?

A number of successful strategies have been tried by many instructors in their classrooms.

Incorporate racial and ethnic diversity in your curriculum—Provide readings and research paper ideas about racially and ethnically diverse topics. Encourage everyone in the class, not just the racially and ethnically diverse students, to pursue these topics.

Invite alumni as guest speakers—Local alumni from your school are often pleased to speak to students and to answer their questions. Make sure your guest speakers represent all of the races and ethnicities in your classroom, if possible. Having them visit and speak throughout the term or semester will help foster an environment in which all people are respected.

Encourage discussions about diversity using great care—Discussing racial and ethnic diversity might make your students uncomfortable. Don't force the issue. However, when you cover the Diversity chapter in *Becoming a Master Student*, there will very likely be occasions when your students will want to talk about diversity. This is positive in that these discussions can lead to an open environment in which it is not difficult to broach difficult topics. However, it is very important not to let such discussions devolve into stereotypical and biased remarks, as can happen under the pretense of good humor.

Jokes, stereotypes, and biases should be addressed in the classroom, if doing so will not cause discomfort to a minority student. Speak to the student or students who make these remarks outside of class, too. See this as an opportunity for critical learning, rather than a reprimand. Help the students understand why stereotypes are inaccurate. Guide them to explore the ways that racism can emerge from an "us and them" mentality. Ask what the point of such a mentality is. If you have a student who continues to make inappropriate remarks in class, consider referring him to a counselor. This is important for the other students in your course and also for the student, who might be setting himself up for difficulty in the workplace and the broader society.

Treat minority students as individuals—Always treat your students as individuals rather than as representatives of a group. Never ask a student to answer a question or speak on behalf of his racial or ethnic group. No individual can speak for others in his "group." There is as much diversity within groups as there is among individuals. Do not look to your diverse students to validate a fact. When discussing issues pertaining to racism, people who don't experience such occurrences often make the person who does encounter them feel uncomfortable.

High School Graduates

Contributed by Ivan Favila and Mary Fleming-Hughes, Counselors, Minority Engineering Recruitment and Retention Program, College of Engineering, University of Illinois at Chicago

When starting a college survival course, you might want to clear up misconceptions or misunderstandings with your students as they make the transition from high school to college.

High School	College
Highly structured	More flexibility
Dependence	Independence
Courses less demanding (requires less time and energy)	Courses more demanding (requires more time and energy)
Student is considered a child, and his parents are held responsible for his actions.	Student is considered an adult, and he is held responsible for his own actions.

Copyright © Houghton Mifflin Company. All rights reserved.

Grades are given to parents, who have access to student's records.	Grades are mailed directly to student.
Student remains in classes for one year.	Student remains in classes for one term.
Four marking periods	One grade reflects entire semester.
Grades might reflect effort, quizzes, attendance, conduct, homework, and teacher's opinion of student.	Grades reflect performance on exams and projects.
Teacher calls parents for conference.	Professor has no interaction with parents.
Teacher seeks out student to offer assistance.	Student must seek out professors for assistance.
Student has daily interaction with teachers and parents.	Student has little or no interaction with teachers and parents.
Counselor meets with student and parents.	Counselor meets with student.
Daily lectures/classroom activities	Lectures are held two or three times a week.
Student does not apply for financial aid.	Student must apply for financial aid to be considered for scholarships, grants, or loans.
School creates social and cultural activities to enhance student's education.	Student must find organizations and activities of interest.
Student can remain in school despite poor academic performance.	Student can be dropped from college for poor academic performance.
Student can be suspended for disobeying rules and regulations.	Student can be dismissed from college permanently for disregarding rules and regulations.

"The High School-to-College Transition"

Article by Clare E. Weinstein, Professor, Educational Psychology; Karalee Johnson, Robert Malloch, Scott Ridley, and Paul Schultz, Graduate Students, Educational Psychology, University of Texas at Austin

Reprinted with the permission of the National Institute for Staff and Organizational Development (NISOD) at the University of Texas at Austin. Innovation Abstracts. September 30, 1988, vol. 10, no. 21.

Community college instructors, developmental specialists, and educational psychologists are becoming increasingly more interested in the nature of the transition between high school and college. Most students enter post-secondary educational settings shortly after they complete their high school studies. However, some come to college years after they have graduated from high school. The educational reference points for both of these groups are often still grounded in their secondary school experiences. This experiential reference point can create problems for students because of the differences between the environments and the demands of high school and college learning settings. If we are committed to helping students to succeed academically, then it is part of our responsibility as educators to help students to make the transition successfully from high school (or from high-school-based expectations) to college.

Using questionnaires and an interview schedule, a study of the differences between secondary and post-secondary educational climates and requirements was conducted as part of the Cognitive Learning Strategies Project located at the University of Texas at Austin. Data was obtained from instructors, students, student affairs specialists, and learning assistance specialists. The results of this study have been pooled with other research findings to identify six categories of differences: (1) academic environment, (2) grading, (3) knowledge acquisition, (4) support, (5) stress, and (6) responsibility.

The following is an edited list of college characteristics highlighting some of the major differences between high school and college:

1. **The academic environment includes differences in operational, or logistical, variables.**
    Instruction is mainly by lecture.
    Reading assignments complement and do not necessarily duplicate lectures.
    There are usually more students at college.

 Copyright © Houghton Mifflin Company. All rights reserved.

There are more social distractions.

Classes meet less frequently and for fewer hours per week.

There is less "busywork."

The tasks often are less structured and less concrete.

Instructors usually are not trained to teach.

Using the library effectively is more important.

Students are held responsible for what they were supposed to have learned in high school and in other courses.

Class discussions often are aimed at raising questions with no clear right or wrong answer.

There is much more emphasis on understanding clearly.

2. **The grading category includes differences in how grades are earned.**

    Harder work is required for earning a grade of A or B.

    The simple completion of an assignment often earns a grade of C or lower.

    Many semester grades are based on only two or three test scores.

    Student progress usually is not closely monitored by instructors.

    Exam questions often are more difficult to predict.

    There are more major writing assignments.

    Essay exams are more common.

3. **The knowledge acquisition category includes differences in how students study and acquire new knowledge and expertise.**

    Instructors rarely suggest ways that students can learn the material.

    Effective reading comprehension skills are more important.

    Taking good notes is more important.

    Few visual and study aids are provided.

    Identifying the main ideas is more important.

    Effective communication skills are more important.

    Students must independently seek additional and supplementary sources of information.

    Students usually must recognize the need for and initiate requests for additional help.

    Students need to monitor their own progress.

    Paying attention in class is more important.

    Studying is more important.

4. **The support category includes the significant differences in the amount of support that students receive.**

    Relationships with family and friends change.

    There is less contact with instructors.

    There is less individual feedback.

    Instructors sometimes are not student-centered.

    There often is more academic competition.

    Behavior problems are not tolerated.

    The environment often is impersonal.

    Students often are given little direction.

5. **The stress category includes differences in the concerns and perceived pressures that students experience.**

    There is an increased workload and faster pace.

    Students are more independent and are held accountable for their behavior.

    It is more difficult to earn high grades.

    An entire course is completed in 14 weeks or fewer.

    Many students experience increased financial responsibilities.

    Many students experience new and often increased social pressures.

    Students are expected to know what they want from college, classes, life, and so on.

Copyright © Houghton Mifflin Company. All rights reserved.

6. **The responsibility category includes the changes associated with a student's role in high school and in college.**

   There are an increased number of choices and decisions to be made.

   More self-evaluation and monitoring are required.

   More independent reading and studying are required.

   Students are more responsible for managing their own time and commitments.

   Students establish and attain their own goals.

   Students determine when they need help and must locate the appropriate resources.

   Students are more responsible to whoever is paying for their education (including themselves!).

   Interest in learning often must be generated by the student.

   Motivation to succeed often must be generated by the student.

Summary—Using information we have gathered about the changes that occur when students make the transition from high school to college can help instructors and student affairs personnel to facilitate the process. Our experience with students in an undergraduate learning-to-learn course indicated that many of them were not aware of the different environmental and task demands that they would face in college. Helping students to become aware of these changes and of the roles that they will need to play in obtaining their education is an important goal for all of us who want to help students maximize their chances of succeeding in college.

International and ESL Students

Contributed by Joel Fleischer, Miami Dade Community College, Miami, FL

Each year the number of international students studying in the United States reaches into the hundreds of thousands. Students who come to our shores as refugees or political asylum-seekers swell the ranks even more. In addition, a significant number of students who are native born speak English as a second language.

These students are challenged to learn a new language and to acquire a second culture as well. What's more, the educational system in our country might differ markedly from what international students expect. The result can be a continuous process of adjustment.

Stages of Cultural Adjustment

This adjustment process might take months to complete. In order to understand this, think of the adjustment that you go through if you move to a different state or province in your own country. You adapt to the new environment; climate changes, variations in diet, and other subtle changes affect the way you act and think. This adjustment is compounded for an international student. Various authors have identified this process as "culture shock" with distinct stages.

Honeymoon stage—This occurs at the outset when students are eager to explore their new culture. Often these students want to please, and they cooperate with you at every level. They might smile and nod in agreement with everything you say, when in fact they might not understand you at all. This characteristically leads to the second phase of cultural adjustment.

Hostility stage—As their frustrations with the new culture increase, students can become angry and stressed. Often they blame the new culture for this discomfort. At this stage, students often lose interest in their work, and in extreme cases, they withdraw. During this stage it is important to be as supportive as possible.

Humor stage—As students adjust to their new surroundings and begin to relax, they can laugh at some of their mistakes—the same mistakes that led to problems during the hostility stage. Now students have made friends and feel more connected to their new surroundings.

   Copyright © Houghton Mifflin Company. All rights reserved.

"At home" stage—Once students feel comfortable in their new host culture and at the same time still feel connected to their native culture, they are "at home." In essence, these students are "bicultural."

Help Students Make the Initial Adjustment

It is essential for educators to recognize special needs. In particular, instructors of college survival courses can use a variety of techniques to help students adapt effectively. The following techniques can assist you, no matter how many international students are enrolled in your course.

Smile—A smile is recognized universally and can help a student feel at ease with you.

Speak more slowly, not more loudly—Many people have a tendency to speak loudly to a person who does not understand English. The person can hear you; he just needs you to speak slowly and clearly.

Learn names—Take time to learn students' names along with the correct pronunciations. Students will appreciate your effort. They, too, are working to learn new pronunciations.

Recognize students—Acknowledging individuals fosters inclusion and a feeling of belonging. Remember that, at first, international students will know few people.

Show interest in differences—Ask international students about their families and native countries. They consider this information important and often enjoy sharing it.

Break information down—Instead of delivering information and ideas in large chunks, experiment with explaining them step by step. Writing down key information can also help.

Prompt for complete information—When filling out forms, international students might inadvertently leave out information. They might not fully understand what needs to go in writing.

Discuss faculty-student relationships—International students can often benefit from talking about their relationships with instructors. Keep in mind that many of these students come from highly formal systems of education and family upbringing. The relatively informal relationship between faculty members and students in your school might come as a surprise. For example, many international students are not used to taking part in class discussions or even raising questions. They might be used to a system in which the teacher's word is final and not open for discussion.

Interpret body language accurately—Some Native American students, for instance, show respect for adults by avoiding eye contact. Sometimes people misinterpret this as exactly the opposite—lack of respect or interest. Instructors can learn to decode such nonverbal behavior and adapt to different styles. Talking about these issues in class can lead to new understanding for the rest of the class as well as for the instructor.

Adapt the Curriculum

The previous suggestions are useful for the initial phases of adjusting to a new culture. Beyond this, it is important for educators to adapt traditional teaching methods. After all, those who teach English as a Second Language (ESL) impart language instruction and also expose students to our wider value system and societal norms. This calls for a flexible approach.

Certain values that international students learn at home can differ radically from what they encounter in our schools. Southeast Asian parents often teach their children that the interests of the family are primary; the individual's interests come second. Completing a class assignment can take a back seat to caring for siblings so that parents can work. This is just one example of the cultural differences, as well as the linguistic challenges, that many international students confront. Such facts call for changes in our curriculum and practices. Several suggested strategies based on concepts from *Becoming a Master Student* follow.

Take a First Step—International students often need an orientation to their new environment. The college survival course is an ideal time to "tell the truth" about what they'll discover. Begin with the physical environment. Guided and self-guided tours are one way to help your students learn the locations of buildings and services. Also make time to review the structure of our higher education system. International

Copyright © Houghton Mifflin Company. All rights reserved.

students might not understand the differences between a technical, two-year school and a four-year university. How degree programs are organized, the concept of a liberal education, the importance attached to grades—all of these might be unfamiliar ideas as well.

Add to this the language of higher education—words such as "semester," "term," "academic advisor," "dropping a course," "freshman," "sophomore," and "major." And don't forget slang: "bombing a test," "flunking out," "cutting class," "jock course," "Greek," "prof," and so on.

Tune in to a new sense of time—North Americans tend to value promptness and time management. However, in other cultures the concept of time has a different meaning and level of importance. Temporal orientations vary across cultures. Some societies focus on the present (Latin America); others look to the past (China).

North American culture is oriented to the future. The value placed on deferred gratification is an illustration: "If I work hard now, I will reap the rewards of future success." Those who do not share this value might be seen as lazy.

Talking about all of this with students can shed new light on the host culture and foster respect for other orientations. It can also help instructors understand why the motivation they seek to instill in students might not "take" with people who have a different outlook on the future.

Choose test items carefully—Test taking is an area in which many international students find it crucial to make adjustments. Objective tests—multiple choice, true/false—have been a mainstay in North America. In contrast, international students might be more versed in subjective examinations such as essay and oral tests. Students who are used to rote memorizing and accepting the instructor's word might flounder when it comes to analyzing or synthesizing material.

What's more, students come from cultures with different literacy traditions. Some cultures emphasize oral tradition, a practice that transmits knowledge through memorizing the *spoken* word. Compare this to the literacy style favored by North Americans, in which students are asked to recall material based on understanding the *written* word.

Take another look at "cheating"—To many international students, cooperation and mutual help are the norm. They might not understand the notions of competitiveness or cheating. Explaining the definitions of honesty and codes of honor can lead to a fascinating discussion. Many Middle Eastern students are used to working in a co-op fashion.

Even a simple demonstration can show how we make assumptions in the absence of the facts. Take an opaque coffee mug and place a fork inside it so that only the tip of the fork is visible. Show this to students and ask them to describe what you are holding. Most will say, "A mug with a spoon." Imagine their surprise when you pull out the fork. This is a concrete way to introduce the topic of assumptions and stereotyping.

Recognize different standards of health and hygiene—These are two dimensions in which cultures differ widely. Both are important to discuss with international students.

One concern for many of them is health care. International students might be amazed at the cost of medical treatment in the United States and might fail to understand the necessity of securing health coverage. This is often the case for students who come from a country with "socialized" medicine.

Personal hygiene is another area to explore. You can explain this issue neutrally from the North American point of view. For example: "Americans are very conscious of smells. We frequently launder our clothes and believe in using deodorants, perfumes, and colognes to mask natural body odor." This approach differs from asking a student to bathe regularly to get rid of an offending odor. Ask students to scan magazines and to notice the number of products designed for hygiene.

Be sensitive to how students manage personal problems—In Western cultures, people seek help from the "outside," such as the services of a professional counselor. In other cultures, this is unthinkable. People from these cultures do not give up their personal locus of control. They quietly handle crises in the context

   Copyright © Houghton Mifflin Company. All rights reserved.

of the family, particularly in cases involving rape, theft, emotional distress, and alcohol or other drug abuse. It might help your students to talk about this difference. Also remember that international students might be missing their traditional family support system.

Point out resources—Exposing international students to campus and community resources is critical. These students might not be familiar with using the library or support services such as academic advising. They might be used to taking required courses rather than choosing electives.

Stress management is a key issue. Explain how students can access counseling both on and off campus. As they go through cultural adjustment, international students might need peer support groups and an understanding ear.

Often international students rely on public transportation. Many will appreciate having route maps and related information.

Enrich Experience Outside the Classroom

Most of the strategies suggested thus far take place in the classroom. Experiences outside the classroom can enhance cross-cultural understanding as well.

Introduce the neighborhood—Neighborhood tours and field trips are a place to start. By exposing students to the wider community, you help them understand the diversity of its people. Visit areas with contrasting racial, ethnic, and religious ties. Stage cultural "treasure hunts" that force interaction between students and local people. ("When you visit this Cuban neighborhood, ask about the common ingredients of their meals.") Take students to a museum so they can get a perspective on local history. See the local government in action as well. Whenever possible, use public transportation and ask guest speakers to give a miniorientation before your group departs.

Promote volunteerism—To underscore the value of volunteering, arrange for students to work in soup kitchens, hospitals, nursing homes, homeless shelters, or for similar organizations.

Promote mentor and tutoring programs—If at all possible, recruit tutors or mentors who can work with students in their first language.

Practice flexibility and ask for feedback—The suggestions in this section offer a start in bridging the gaps of language and culture. Beyond these, use a variety of teaching styles. Ask for feedback from students to make sure you are meeting their needs. In so doing, you go a long way in assisting their cultural adaptation.

Returning Adults

Historically, our educational systems have been geared to lecture. Although the content taught in higher education differs from the content taught to younger students, most of the models of teaching and learning used are fundamentally the same. As the percentage of older students returning to school increases, more and more educators are learning to adapt their teaching to meet the needs of these students. Often, the strategies that successfully involve older students can enhance the learning of traditional-age students as well. This section contains ideas and techniques that have proved useful for all students, particularly returning adults.

Be sensitive to concerns outside of school—Returning adults are often managing full and challenging lives in addition to attending school. Jobs, children, and spouses require time and energy that can interfere with educational commitments. Discuss childcare facilities, car-pooling information, and other resources that are available. Encourage students to form support groups to share ideas about particular problems. Organize study groups during the first week of class. Teach time-management skills. Ask students to discuss how the people in their lives can be part of a team that promotes their success.

Copyright © Houghton Mifflin Company. All rights reserved.

Stress practical benefits—Older students in particular are interested in how they will be able to use what they learn at college in real-life situations. Students will be far more interested in a theory if they learn practical applications along with it. They will generally care more about answering the question "How can I use this?" than the question "Which theorist developed that idea?"

Point out the relevance of what you are teaching to life outside the classroom. Ask students to think about how they are going to put what they are learning to work in their lives. In discussions and on quizzes, ask application questions as well as literal and comprehension questions. Take field trips. Use problem-solving activities and actual case studies. Expand laboratory programs. Review your curriculum and eliminate courses that are outdated and material that is irrelevant.

Affirm experience—Older students generally have a greater abundance and wider variety of life experiences than younger students. Ask them for examples to illustrate a point. Encourage them to talk about, and even teach, what they already know.

Many adult learners minimize what they already know. They might be overly concerned about their deficiencies and how much they have to learn and relearn. These students might not realize the value of what they have already experienced. Acknowledge and respect the fact that they have a great deal to contribute to the classroom.

Allow students to express their anxiety about returning to school. Opportunities to air concerns can relieve insecurity and fear about this new experience. They can also serve to create an awareness that many other new students have similar emotions.

Beware of experience—Older students have had more time to solidify their values, belief systems, and expectations. They might resist experimenting with new strategies and accepting new ideas. Look for exercises that offer students opportunities to examine their biases, question their assumptions, and clarify their values. Have group discussions that explore new ways of thinking about things. Invite students to be open to accepting alternative points of view.

Suggest that students temporarily put aside what they "know" and approach an unfamiliar idea with the question "What if that were true?" This approach might bring new ideas to light. New ideas are built on previous ones. Potentially damaging ideas that are examined with an open, accepting, and inquisitive attitude will not harm us and will wither away naturally. Beneficial breakthroughs are born out of forgetting what we "know." Use brainstorming to help students see that there are many more possibilities in the world than the ones they can think of by themselves.

Discuss the advantages of not finding "the" answer to a question. Putting aside answers in order to remain engaged in an inquiry often leads to acceptable alternatives and innovative directions.

Integrate students—Returning adults have a tendency to form groups with other returning adults. This is a problem only if it is done all of the time. During exercises, devise ways to form groups that contain a variety of students. All students benefit from interacting with people who have different experiences and values and with others of different cultures, ages, and genders.

Use guest speakers—Invite guest speakers who completed their education as returning adults and who are involved in areas that students find interesting. Ask students for suggestions about which guest speakers they think would be beneficial. Alumni from your course and from your school make especially credible models. Ask guest speakers to relate their current careers (and lives) to their educational experience.

Reinforce self-responsibility—The previous education experience of most returning students was teacher dependent. Students were told what to do, when to do it, and also precisely how to do it. Some adult learners bring this passive attitude with them when they return to school. We can be careful not to reinforce that attitude. As students become increasingly more responsible for their education, they become more involved and committed. Ask them to write their educational goals, share them with the class, and relate what they do in their daily routines to achieve those goals. They are likely to discover others who have similar goals. Invite students to participate fully in class through exercises, conversations and sharing, and writing Discovery and Intention Statements. You can also give students responsibility for evaluating their own performance.

   Copyright © Houghton Mifflin Company. All rights reserved.

Use contracts—Students can design their own education in ways that best meet their individual needs and current circumstances. By using learning contracts, students are less likely to feel victimized and are more likely to be proactive. They can make choices about what outcomes they desire, which tasks they will complete to achieve a particular grade, how they will participate, what resources they will use, and how they will be evaluated.

Have flexible scheduling—Nontraditional students appreciate being able to take a course in the evening or on weekends. If they are in school part-time, it is frustrating for them to have to wait an entire year before a course that they need or want is offered again. Find out what course schedules make the most sense.

Encourage outside support—Invite partners, children, and others who play significant roles in students' lives to visit the campus. Design programs that help them feel comfortable and show them ways that they can support the students' efforts.

Gay and Lesbian Students

Gay and lesbian students have unique needs and concerns and might face greater challenges in college than their heterosexual peers. Although research suggests that more than 10 percent of the population is gay or lesbian, this population is often not visible and thus might be underserved on campus. Instructors should be aware of on- and off-campus resources for gays and lesbians and ready to offer institutional support for them. This article discusses some specific concerns of gay and lesbian students and suggests resources that instructors can offer.

Coming Out—"Coming out" is a process of achieving self-acceptance in a world that is largely ignorant about gays and lesbians and often hostile to them. Gay and lesbian students come out to themselves, first, when they accept their sexuality. They might also choose to come out to friends and family, and to the campus community by discussing their sexual orientation with teachers, in papers, or in classroom discussions. By coming out, homosexual students discover that they are not alone. Coming out is a courageous act and should always be treated with respect. Instructors can make coming out less difficult for students by encouraging a climate of tolerance and support, and by discussing gay and lesbian issues in class.

Marginalization—"Marginalization" is the process by which the dominant culture pushes minority cultures to the margins of society through exclusion. It is a problem for all minority groups. Even those homosexual students who have come out might feel intimidated in social settings in which heterosexuality is assumed. In class discussions, avoid "heterosexism."—the attitude that assumes that all individuals are heterosexual. Also avoid labeling individuals as straight or gay and perpetuating myths about the causes of homosexuality or supposed characteristics of gays and lesbians. Strive for inclusion of all students and for the deconstruction of stereotypes and attitudes that keep homosexuals and other minorities on the outside.

Health—Substance abuse, nicotine addiction, suicide, and sexually transmitted diseases are all disproportionately severe problems in the gay and lesbian community. To help prevent health problems among this population, educate your students about campus resources that are available to them, such as counseling and health centers. Many counselors and medical professionals have received training on how these issues affect gay men and lesbians, and can therefore be a valuable source of support for them.

Finding a voice—Direct students to the library for gay and lesbian newspapers, directories of gay and lesbian organizations, and research on gay and lesbian culture. The Web is a particularly good source of information on gay and lesbian issues and groups. Try **http://www.gay.com** for information about news, activism, relationships, health and fitness, finance, and travel. Or do a web search on "gay support" or "lesbian support."

Copyright © Houghton Mifflin Company. All rights reserved.

If a gay or lesbian student believes he or she has been discriminated against, campus antidiscrimination policies and local, state, or federal laws might provide avenues of recourse. Check your institution's web site for information on its policies, and see the Gay Politics and Law site at **http://www.indiana. edu ~ glbtpol/** for information on laws and legal resources of interest to the general gay and lesbian community.

Students with Disabilities

The Americans with Disabilities Act and Service to Students

We would like to thank Sharon Hinson Davis, Ed.D., R.D., L.D., for sharing her expertise and experience with us in this section. Sharon was a selected presenter at the Student Success Course Colloquium in Toronto, Canada, in 1996 at which she presented on this topic. Sharon is the assistant director of the University of Arkansas Medical Sciences/Veterans Affairs Medical Center Dietetic Internship, Little Rock, AR. She is also an assistant professor in the Department of Nutrition and Dietetics, College of Health Related Professions, University of Arkansas for Medical Sciences. Sharon has worked at the VA Medical Center in Little Rock and in education for 25 years.

The number of students with a disability who receive a full secondary school education and who participate in a college education has increased in recent decades primarily because of (a) the passage of the Americans with Disabilities Act (ADA), which defines the rights, coverage, and eligibility requirements for citizens with disabilities; (b) the influx of older learners returning to college with accompanying disabilities; and (c) advances in medicine and technology.

The ADA (Public Law 101-336) is based on the Rehabilitation Act of 1973 (Public Law 93-112). Four definitions are essential for a clear understanding of the ADA in higher education.

Under Section Ib(3) of the ADA, a disabled person is defined as (a) an individual with a physical or mental impairment that substantially limits one or more major life activities, and (b) having a record of such an impairment or (b) being regarded as having such an impairment. "Major life activity" is interpreted as being able to care for oneself and [to] perform common tasks such as walking, seeing, hearing, speaking, breathing, learning, and working (EEOC, 1992). "A qualified individual with a disability" (Section 101[8]) has (a) the requisite skills, experience, education, and other academically related requirements for admission to a program; (b) can fulfill, with or without reasonable accommodations, the essential requirements/functions of students at each stage of his education; and (c) does not pose a direct threat of substantial harm to the health or safety of others. Finally, "essential requirements/functions" are those physical abilities, mental abilities, skills, attitudes, and behaviors that students in educational programs must evidence, demonstrate, or perform at each stage of their education (Essex-Sorlie, 1994).

The conditions presented by a student might or might not be defined as a disability based on state statutes, the courts, and previous case law. Those students with a record of the disability as a result of public school identification or of an assessment done by qualified professionals have little difficulty providing the college or university with the documentation necessary to indicate that a disability exists.

The student is responsible for documenting a disability and requesting accommodations. Colleges and universities do not have a duty to inquire into the existence of a disability and are specifically prohibited from making inquiries (Milani, 1996).

Students entering colleges or universities can acknowledge a disability, provide documentation, sign up with the disability support services, and request accommodations. The expectations of services and accommodations by these individuals (and their parents) presently exceed those of disabled students in past years. Many of these students have developed extensive coping mechanisms and deal successfully with the limitations that their disabilities have imposed. On the other hand, students might not be aware of or acknowledge a disability due to the stigma attached. These students might be known only as poor test takers or poor students. Many disabilities are not identified until the student leaves the slower pace of high school and the supportive environment of home.

 Copyright © Houghton Mifflin Company. All rights reserved.

Disabilities can be visible or invisible. Although research studies divide types of disabilities differently, they generally fall into one of five categories: sensory, physical, learning, behavior, and chronic health. Sensory and physical disabilities are most often thought of when disabilities are discussed. However, the number of students with learning disabilities consistently makes up 23 percent of the total number of students with disabilities and might require the most complex accommodations. Many students with physical or sensory disabilities provide their own accommodations. Their primary concern might be accessibility to the campus, classrooms, restrooms, and labs.

Students with disabilities do not have common characteristics, nor do they have the same types of disabilities. Disabilities occur without respect to age, sex, intellect, physical characteristics, race, economic status, social standing, or geographical location. Therefore, each student, even those with the same disability, will have specific and unique needs. The best way to determine the individuality of his requirements is to ask the student requesting accommodations. A frank and open discourse between the student and the instructor is the foundation of a successful education experience.

The institution is responsible for the following:

1. A campus that is accessible to students with disabilities
2. Development of policies and procedures that include (a) a definition of disability, (b) a statement of eligibility for services to include a medical/professional documentation of a disability, (c) a statement on confidentiality stating who should or should not be informed of the disability, and (d) a description of prohibited discriminatory actions in admissions and readmissions
3. Providing and paying for the requested accommodation if the device is used principally to fulfill essential educational requirements and is not used throughout the student's daily activities. The institution is not obligated to provide the most expensive accommodation and is allowed to supply one that will meet the needs of the student
4. Providing education to administrators, staff, and faculty concerning the ADA, resources available, and teaching methods specific for students with disabilities

The student is responsible for maintaining a positive attitude regarding his disability, the quality of his education, and his own learning. No one else will be able to gain knowledge or acquire skills for him. In addition, he is responsible for the following:

1. Documenting a disability by pursuing and paying for a workup and diagnosis from a qualified professional
2. Requesting needed accommodations in writing
3. Requesting accommodations within an appropriate/reasonable time frame (An institution might have to purchase equipment, or an instructor might have to develop materials.)
4. Demonstrating a willingness to negotiate on types of accommodations or materials
5. Following college or university rules related to the use of the accommodations provided
6. Seeking information actively, asking questions, listening, and being resourceful

Teaching Tips for the Instructor

1. Become knowledgeable about the ADA and the institution's policies and procedures on students with disabilities and confidentiality. Visit the disability support services and meet the resource people who can provide services to students with disabilities and to you as an instructor. Review the accommodations that are available in the disability support services office and in other departments such as the computer lab. Add disability support services staff to the list of guest speakers for your college survival course. If your facility does not have a disability support services office or an individual who is responsible for those functions, visit those of a nearby college or university.
2. Identify clearly the requirements and/or functions essential for successful completion of the class. Teaching methods that will aid all students in your class include the goals/objectives of the class, a list of assignments, examples of acceptable assignments, a method or example of evaluation for each assignment, a vocabulary list, the requirements for each grade level, and attendance requirements.

Copyright © Houghton Mifflin Company. All rights reserved.

Constructive feedback is vital on all assignments. There should be no surprises for the student. DO NOT ASSUME ANYTHING.

3. When a student with a disability enrolls in your class, you might infer that the student meets the basic admission policies of the institution. While the student will have completed high school, he will have a disability and possibly also have the same problems as other entering freshmen—poor study habits, poor reading and writing skills, and so on. Do not let the disability of the student overshadow either the needs or the talents of the student.

4. If the student does not acknowledge a disability or request accommodations in the class, the instructor is not to inquire into the existence of a disability or offer accommodations. The student must then meet the academic and attendance requirements of the class. However, during the class on how to become a master student, the student can be made aware of student and disability support services on campus.

5. When a student with a disability requests accommodations, provide these accommodations as discreetly as possible. Even when you are accommodating students with very visible disabilities, other members of the class might feel cheated. The instructor does not owe other members of the class an explanation of the accommodations provided. However, if accommodations are instructor controlled, such as extended test-taking periods, oral exams, or requests for take-home tests, the instructor might consider extending the accommodation to all members of the class.

6. Use a problem-solving approach to identify and implement reasonable accommodations for the student with disabilities after the obligation to accommodate has been established. The best way to determine needs is to ask the student who is requesting accommodations. Do not assume that you know what accommodations this student needs—disabilities are as individual as the students who have them. In addition, you might review the recommendations made by the specialist who evaluated the student for documentation of disabilities and check with the disability support services or an appropriate representative on campus.

7. Accommodations generally fall into one or more of the following categories: (a) assistance by personnel, for example, a reader or interpreter; (b) technology such as a computer/laptop or assistive listening devices; (c) materials including large print or Braille materials/books; and (d) instructor-controlled activities such as extra time for test taking or schedule changes. Many accommodations can be provided at the discretion of the instructor. Provide instructor-controlled accommodations that have been requested by students in a reasonable and timely manner.

8. Document and date the requests made by the student with a disability and the accommodations provided by the institution and/or instructor. A good-faith effort to work with the student is essential to avoid litigation.

9. If possible, locate a faculty or staff person with a similar disability and discuss teaching methods with him or her. *It is vital to use extreme caution in this situation.* Always ask the student's permission before introducing him to another individual with a similar disability or setting up a mentoring program. You might also need to check with your administration for permission or advice on how to proceed.

10. If and when the occasion arises, outline in writing the responsibilities of both the instructor and the student with disabilities and negotiate a mutually satisfying agreement.

References

Americans with Disabilities Act of 1990 (Public Law 101-336).

Bowman, O. J., and D. K. Marzouk. "Implementing the Americans with Disabilities Act of 1990 in Higher Education." *The American Journal of Occupational Therapy* 46(6): 521–533.

Davis, Sharon H. "*The Americans with Disabilities Act: Impact on Dietetic Education.*" Dissertation in partial fulfillment of the requirements for completion of the Doctorate of Education, University of Arkansas–Fayetteville, May 1994.

Copyright © Houghton Mifflin Company. All rights reserved.

Henderson, C. *College Freshmen with Disabilities: A Statistical Profile*. Washington, DC: American Council on Education, HEATH Resource Center. (ERIC Document Reproduction Service No. ED 354 792).

Milani, Adam. "Disabled Students in Higher Education: Administrative and Judicial Enforcement of Disability Law." *Journal of College and University Law* 22(4): 989–1143.

Yuker, H. E. *Attitudes Toward Persons with Disabilities*. New York: Springer, 1988.

Resources for Visually Challenged Students

College Survival and the *Becoming a Master Student* program have a commitment to the entire first-year student community. The Tenth Edition of *Becoming a Master Student* will be available from Recording for the Blind and Dyslexic. If you know professors or students who wish to obtain the audio version of the text, please have them contact Recording for the Blind and Dyslexic at 800-221-4792. The audio version is free of charge to members.

Captioning Services

A list of companies providing captioning services is available from the Instructional Television and Media Services Department of the National Technical Institute for the Deaf. The department suggests that if you plan to have a program captioned, first define your needs and then obtain price quotes and references from at least two contractors.

To receive this list or for more information, call or write to the Instructional Television and Media Services Department, National Technical Institute for the Deaf, Rochester Institute of Technology, P.O. Box 9887, Rochester, NY 14623, 716-475-6581.

Students with Learning Challenges

Contributed by Bill Jones and Bill Racherbaumer, Monterey Peninsula College, Monterey, CA

Over the years, the term "learning disability" has been defined in different ways by numerous government agencies, educational organizations, and school districts. Although most definitions include several common elements of learning disabilities, the label is often misunderstood and continues to generate many misconceptions. The resources given at the end of this section direct you to more information about learning disabilities.

All of us have strengths and deficiencies in the way we process information. On a continuum, some of our deficiencies interfere more with our learning than others. Most of us are able to compensate and balance our learning processes so that our deficiencies do not noticeably interfere with our ability to read, write, comprehend, solve math problems, and so on.

People with deficiencies that lead to a more severe and noticeable impact on academic performance are said to have learning disabilities. It is a matter of degree only. In other words, all of us have unique strengths, weaknesses, learning styles, and ways of processing information. The following strategies that are effective for teaching students with learning disabilities are equally effective for teaching any student.

Maintain high and realistic expectations—Establishing high and realistic expectations for students contributes to their success. This is especially true of students with learning disabilities. We are doing ourselves and students a disservice if we overreact to a disability and lower our expectations for achievement. A student with learning disabilities might require more time or need to use different strategies to be successful. Expectations of high performance standards can be maintained, and performance most certainly can be extraordinary.

Accept mistakes—Very few of us perform a skill perfectly the first time we try it. Rarely do we fully comprehend a complex concept when we first hear about it. Learning involves trial and error, practice,

Copyright © Houghton Mifflin Company. All rights reserved.

repetition, and mistakes. Mistakes provide feedback so that we can learn, grow, and improve. Failing or making mistakes might indicate the need for more practice, or it might suggest that we try a different strategy. Academic failure is not a reflection of personal worth.

Communicate self-responsibility—One of the most helpful decisions any student can make is to accept responsibility for creating value in his own education. Too often, having a learning disability is used as an excuse by students, parents, and educators to transfer the responsibility for learning to someone other than the student. Educational institutions and teachers are responsible for meeting the needs of students by providing appropriate educational opportunities. The responsibility for learning rests with the student.

Use multisensory teaching techniques—Say it, show it, and do it. Follow the seven-part course structure outlined in Part II of this manual. Stress the "Use your body" memory techniques described in the Memory chapter of *Becoming a Master Student*. Like all students, those with learning disabilities can learn to compensate for deficiencies by combining and balancing stronger learning processes and modalities.

Individualize learning—Be sensitive to the preferred perceiving and processing modalities of students. If, for example, a student needs more time to take a test, schedule special test-taking sessions or allow oral tests. Use small groups and peer tutoring. Encourage students to investigate how they learn and to give you suggestions about how best to individualize their instruction.

Encourage candid communication—Students can be prepared to discuss their learning disabilities with fellow students, teachers, counselors, and administrators. They can be assertive about having their needs met. They can request special testing formats, find out if there are alternatives to written assignments, arrange for teaching assistants and tutors to provide extra help, structure unique study groups, learn about services and resources that are available on campus and in the community, establish personal support networks, and educate others about the nature of their learning disability. Some students find it helpful to meet with instructors and counselors on a weekly basis, even if it is just to say hello. The more understanding that can be generated about learning disabilities, the easier it is for everyone, including the student, to promote individual success.

Encourage planning—Long-range academic planning and career counseling help students choose paths that are compatible with their strengths and, consequently, help ensure success.

Suggest taking fewer class hours—If students can accept that it will take more time than they had planned to complete their formal education, they might be able to improve their chances for success. They can take fewer classes each term and have more flexibility to balance easier classes with more difficult ones.

Promote compensatory techniques—Resources and strategies that can be beneficial include using tape recorders, finding a study partner in each class, forming a study group, attending all classes, asking questions in class, sitting in the front row, buying textbooks in advance, visiting instructors and classrooms prior to registration, listening to audio versions of textbooks, touring the library, and locating test files. A group brainstorm might generate many more helpful ideas. Consult experts. You are not and should not be alone.

Student Athletes

Athletes are unique learners, contending with the usual concerns of students, such as social commitments, challenging academic pursuits, and personal/family problems, and also with the pressures of competition, the possibility of injury, physical fatigue, and tremendous time-management challenges. In addition, some (though not all) athletes arrive at their post-secondary experience underprepared academically. Many instructors see athletes as disinterested academic observers who are protected by their coaches and the school's athletics department. Misconceptions include the following: athletes care only about sports. They

 Copyright © Houghton Mifflin Company. All rights reserved.

are inherently not very smart. They have more muscle than brain. Athletes make it through the college or university experience on favors rather than academic effort. Gaining national sports recognition is more important to most athletes than gaining any measurable amount of knowledge or skill from the post-secondary experience. Right? Wrong!!

Athletes are often motivated, controlled, disciplined, and physically and spiritually connected individuals. Many athletes are kinesthetic learners, and as such they are easily distracted and prone to multiple stimuli overload—the result of having overactive sensory receptors. Instructors should allow all students, particularly athletes, to stand and stretch at periodic intervals (usually every 20 minutes).

Teachers often complain that their students, especially athletes, have frustratingly low attention spans. Many of us learn in 20-minute spans, with the greatest information absorption occurring at the beginning and end of each attention span peak. In other words, we pay attention at minutes one and 20 and everything in the middle is lost, to a lesser or greater degree. Learning for athletes is greatly facilitated when the instructor breaks the lecture into smaller units.

In order to better facilitate the academic success of athletes, multisensory, active learning strategies are recommended. Accelerated learning techniques provide some interesting and exciting alternatives for athletes. Students are encouraged to learn in high-energy environments that reward initiative and boost self-esteem. Lessons are presented with a multidimensional approach that accommodates different learning styles, speeds, and needs.

Practical Hints for Teaching Athletes

- Let them know that it's OK not to be the "hot shot" in class.

- Make sure, though, that you make room for more reticent, introverted students to participate if they want to.

- Become the classroom coach, constantly and consistently encouraging active learning. Let your student athlete stand in class or during tutorial sessions. Walking around the room is OK, too. Don't insist, though, that every student should do this.

- Open a conversation with the athlete regarding academic attitudes and goals. You might be surprised to find out that you are the first instructor to do so.

- Discuss time management. How many hours of athletic responsibilities does the student athlete have in a week? Where can he consolidate, prune, and save energy? How can he utilize travel time to away games in order to review notes, listen to lecture tapes, and so on?

- Reinforce the Power Process "Be here now." Let your student athlete know that daydreaming is normal. Teach the student how not to get involved in a mental tug-of-war when daydreaming begins.

- Tell the athlete to attend class. Travel and practice schedules might lead to an unavoidable absence. Make videotapes of your classes available to all students who have to miss classes.

- Tell the athlete to communicate often with instructors. There is no better way to dispel the "dumb jock" myth than to personally exhibit an interest in learning.

- Use sports analogies. Recall is greatly facilitated for many athletes by image generation, especially if the subject can be related to a sports image.

- Suggest that athletes practice relaxation exercises. Conscious relaxation in the classroom can aid in controlling those constantly firing sensory receptors.

- Be flexible. At times, the student athlete might need to disregard the text organization in an effort to learn the material in an "easy-to-difficult" format. Remember that athletic training does not begin with the most difficult physical maneuver, so why should learning?

- Move around and use your hands when explaining concepts and procedures.

- Send the student athlete to the chalkboard or marker board as often as the lesson allows.

Copyright © Houghton Mifflin Company. All rights reserved.

- Use basic Montessori methods when instructing student athletes.
  - **Input**—Monitor reception of stimuli from the environment.
  - **Integration**—Associate new material and make connections with what the student already knows.
  - **Output**—Use physical (gestures) and vocal expression of new ideas.
  - **Feedback**—Monitor output and adjust the system for better response.
- Finally, consider this idea. Many students report that simply knowing the time of day they were born is a great asset in trying to achieve maximum academic effectiveness. Think about it. What is the first thing that babies do after birth? They cry and then sleep. Our biological clocks are set at birth. Many students report that they experience downtime shortly after the time of day that they were born. They avoid studying during these hours as it is usually not productive. Sounds strange, and it works!

Students at Christian-Affiliated Colleges

Many of the Power Processes, success strategies, and ideas discussed in *Becoming a Master Student* are aligned with Christian principles. This section suggests ways to incorporate scripture into your lesson plans. A special thanks is extended to Marita Morgan of Oral Roberts University, Tulsa, OK, for contributing the scriptural examples.

Scripture can give depth and credibility to the messages in *Becoming a Master Student*. The events and relationships recorded in the Bible have universal meaning. The teachings of the Bible can have significant relevance in our daily lives. Incorporating these teachings into your course can help students focus on the content. Learning can be reinforced through exposure to scriptural examples of key concepts. Students can increase their appreciation for how Christian perspectives of life can be applied to their practical goals of being successful in school.

Make It Meaningful

In some circles, *Becoming a Master Student* has been accused of promoting humanistic ideals, New Age doctrines, or Eastern mysticism. The first Power Process in the text, "Ideas are tools," suggests that students should not believe any of the ideas in the book. The techniques and principles included in the text have been collected from many different sources. No doctrine or ideology is endorsed. Not even the practical techniques and strategies are endorsed. The text suggests experimenting with all of these, adopting what is effective, and putting the rest on the shelf. Students can use their own value systems as the criteria for selecting those ideas and techniques that they will use.

Just about any issue, concern, objection, or criticism can be turned into a valuable discussion that helps students clarify Christian values in their daily lives. For example, if the New Age concern arises, students can be asked to consider this question: "What are the messages of New Age ideology, and how are they similar to or in what ways do they contradict Christian principles?"

Another valuable discussion can be generated concerning the meaning of the Power Process "I create it all." Is this a prideful attitude denying that God creates all things? Or can the concept be perceived as being aligned with Joshua 24:15: "Choose you this day whom you will serve . . ."? Does it simply mean that we are responsible for all of our behaviors? Does it mean that we choose our actions and reactions, that we choose which ideas to incorporate into our lives, and, in this sense, that we "create" our experience of the world? How does having been redeemed and forgiven allow us to design, build, and respond to life differently than if we had not been redeemed and forgiven?

You can always look for different ways to use Scripture to begin conversations and sharing, to design exercises, and to create test questions. A seed for conversations and sharing, for example, could be to ask

    Copyright © Houghton Mifflin Company. All rights reserved.

how John 8:32 is related to the Discovery Wheel: "You shall know the truth and the truth shall set you free." How does this relate to II Corinthians 5:17: "If any man is in Christ, he is a new creature, the old things passed away; behold new things have come." By discussing these passages, students can focus on the realization that being "in Christ" involves telling the truth. This First Step of self-analysis helps us see our strengths and weaknesses. The next step is to become a "new creature" through changing our habits. You could even have students rename each Power Process using a Biblical verse. Asking students to rename concepts using Biblical references helps reinforce the ideas, gives students more ownership of the concepts, and enhances their ability to articulate the principles of their faith.

Another assignment could be "Discuss the memory techniques that are illustrated when Peter remembered the words Jesus had spoken: 'Before the rooster crows, you will disown me three times.'" The answer could include talking about the memory techniques "Make it meaningful," "Create associations," "Remember something else," and "Combine memory techniques" from the text.

Scriptural Connections to the Text

Scripture related to material in *Becoming a Master Student* can be used as seeds for conversations and sharing. Assignments can include researching and writing about Biblical quotes that connect the ideas and techniques in the text to Christian teachings. Ask how one particular Scripture is aligned with several different ideas in the text. Following are a few examples that relate to various key topics:

Goal setting—I Corinthians 9:24–25: "Do you not know that those who run in a race all run, but only one receives the prize? Run in such a way that you might win. And everyone who competes in the games exercises self-control in all things. They then do it to receive a perishable wrath, but we are imperishable."

Goal setting—Jeremiah 29:11: "For I know the plans that I have for you, declares the Lord, plans for welfare and not for calamity to give you a future and a hope."

Discovery Wheel—II Corinthians 5:17: "If any man is in Christ, he is a new creature; the old things passed away; behold new things have come."

Tell the truth—Proverbs 28:13: "He who conceals his transgressions will not prosper, but he who confesses and forsakes them will find compassion."

Discovery Statements—Ephesians 4:25: "Laying aside falsehood, speak truth, each one of you, with his neighbor, for we are members of one another."

Intention Statements—Proverbs 16:3: "Commit to the Lord whatever you do, and your plans will succeed."

Master students—2 Timothy 2:15: "Study to show thyself approved unto God, a worker who does not need to be ashamed, rightly dividing the work of truth."

Money—Ephesians 4:19: "My God shall supply all your needs according to His riches in glory in Christ Jesus."

Time management—Ecclesiastes 3:1–8: "There is an appointed time for everything, and there is a time for every event under heaven. A time to give birth, and a time to die. A time to plant, and a time to uproot what is planted. A time to kill, and a time to heal. . . ."

Time management—Ephesians 5:15–17: "Be careful how you walk, not as unwise men, but as wise, making the most of your time. . . ."

Time management—Proverbs 16:9–10: "The mind of a man plans his way, but the Lord directs his steps."

Goals—Psalm 37:4: "Delight yourself in the Lord, and He will give you the desires of your heart."

"Be here now"—Hebrews 2:1: "We must pay more careful attention, therefore, to what we have heard so that we do not drift away."

Copyright © Houghton Mifflin Company. All rights reserved.

Memory—John 14:26: "The helper, the Holy Spirit, whom the Father will send in My name, He will teach you all things, and bring to your remembrance all that I said to you."

"Love your problems"—Matthew 5:44: "But I say to you, love your enemies, bless those who curse you, do good to those who hate you, and pray for those who spitefully use you and persecute you."

Reading—Daniel 5:8: "All the King's wise men came in, but they could not read the inscription or make known its interpretation to the King."

Note taking—Isaiah 30:8-9: "Now go, write it on a tablet before them and inscribe it on a scroll, that it might serve as a witness forever. For this is a rebellious people, false sons, sons who refuse to listen to the instructions of the Lord."

"I create it all"—Matthew 15:11, 19: "Not what enters into the mouth defiles a man, but what proceeds out of the mouth, this defiles the man. For out of the heart come evil thoughts, murders, adulteries, fornications, thefts, false witness, slanders."

"I create it all"—Joshua 24:15: "Choose for yourselves this day whom you will serve. . . ."

Study groups—Ecclesiastes 4:9-10: "Two are better than one because they have a good return for their labor. For if either of them falls, the one will lift up his companion. But woe to the one who falls when there is not another to lift him up."

Study groups—I Thessalonians 5:11: "Encourage one another, and build one another up. . . ."

Testing—II Corinthians 13:5: "Test yourselves to see if you are in the faith: examine yourselves!"

Testing—James 1:5-6: "If any of you lacks wisdom, let him ask of God, who gives to all men generously and without reproach, and it will be given to him. But let him ask in faith without any doubting. . . ."

Anxiety—II Timothy 1:7: "For God has not given you a spirit of fear, but a spirit of love, power, and a sound mind."

Anxiety—I Corinthians 14:33: "For God is not a God of confusion but of peace."

Creativity—Isaiah 40:28-31: "God . . . the creator . . . does not become weary . . . He gives strength . . . increases power . . . those who wait for the Lord will gain new strength; they will mount up with wings like eagles, they will run and not get tired, they will walk and not become weary."

Communication—Hebrews 10:24: "Let us consider how to stimulate one another to love and do good deeds . . . encouraging one another."

Relationships—Philippians 2:3-4: "Do nothing from selfishness or empty conceit, but with humility of mind let each of you regard one another as more important than himself; do not merely look out for your own personal interests, but also for the interests of others."

Relationships—Matthew 5:44: "Jesus said, love your enemies, and pray for those who persecute you. . . ."

Relationships—Ephesians 4:32: "Be kind and compassionate to one another, forgiving each other, just as in Christ God forgave you."

Relationships—I Corinthians 10:24: "Let no one seek his own good, but that of his neighbor."

Relationships—Philippians 2:14: "Do all things without grumbling or disputing."

Relationships—I Corinthians 13:1-13: "Love is patient . . . kind . . . not jealous. . . . Love does not brag . . . is not arrogant . . . does not act unbecomingly . . . does not seek its own . . . is not provoked . . . does not take into account wrongs suffered, rejoices in truth, never fails." (Many of these statements can be translated into positive Intention Statements.)

"Employ your word"—Proverbs 10:9: "He who walks with integrity walks securely, but he who perverts his ways will become known."

   Copyright © Houghton Mifflin Company. All rights reserved.

Diversity—Matthew 37:39: "You shall love your neighbor as yourself."

"Choose your conversations and your community"—Ephesians 5:12: "Do not let any unwholesome talk come out of your mouths, but only what is helpful for building others up according to their needs, that it might benefit those who listen."

"Choose your conversations and your community"—Philippians 4:8: "Finally, brothers, whatever is true, whatever is noble, whatever is right, whatever is admirable—if anything is excellent or praise worthy—think about such things."

Knowledge—Ecclesiastes 12:9–10: "In addition to being a wise man, the Preacher also taught the people knowledge, and he pondered, searched out, and arranged many proverbs. The Preacher sought to find delightful words and to write words of truth correctly."

Health—I Corinthians 3:16–17: "Do you know that you are the temple of God, and that the Spirit of God dwells in you? If any man destroys the temple of God, God will destroy him, for the temple of God is holy, and that is what you are."

Health—Romans 12:1–2: "I urge you therefore, brethren, by the mercies of God, to present your bodies a living and holy sacrifice, acceptable to God, which is your spiritual service of worship. And do not be conformed to this world, but be transformed by the renewing of your mind, that you might prove what the will of God is, that which is good and acceptable and perfect."

"Be it"—Philippians 3:13–16: "Forgetting what lies behind and reaching forward to what lies ahead, I press on toward the goal for the prize of the upward call of God in Christ Jesus. Let us, therefore, as many as are perfect, have this attitude; and if in anything you have a different attitude, God will reveal that also to you; however, let us keep living by that same standard to which we have attained."

"Be it"—Proverbs 4:25–27: "Let your eyes look directly ahead, and let your gaze be fixed straight in front of you. Watch the path of your feet, and all your ways will be established. Do not turn to the right nor to the left; turn your foot from evil."

"Be it"—Proverbs 23:7: "For as he thinks within himself, so he is."

Attitudes—Philippians 4:6–7: "Be anxious for nothing, but in everything by prayer and supplication with thanksgiving let your requests be made known to God. And the peace of God, which surpasses all comprehension, shall guard your hearts and your minds in Christ Jesus."

Attitudes—Hebrews 4:12: "For the word of God is living and active and . . . able to judge the thoughts and intentions of the heart."

Do something you can't—Ephesians 4:13: "I can do all things through Christ who strengthens me."

(NOTE: Scriptures were taken from the New American Standard Version of the Bible and the New International Version.)

Student Retention

This section provides a campuswide perspective on creating a welcoming and supportive experience for your students who have just arrived at college. However, a college survival course is not likely to resolve all of the difficult issues facing your students if there are other aspects of the academic, social, or physical environments or agencies for support that need to be assessed and improved.

American College Testing indicated decades ago that in order to improve retention, a college or university campus must improve service at every point at which the student interacts with the institution. This section allows you to consider whether your campus has areas for improvement and also gives you a chance to celebrate what you are doing well.

Copyright © Houghton Mifflin Company. All rights reserved.

Students often leave school when the costs outweigh the perceived benefits. As consumers, it isn't the big issues that irritate us as much as the insidious frustrations. These could be easily changed if someone on campus with a service-to-student point of view notices and brings them to the attention of the people responsible. Perhaps you are the person who will finally remedy a situation that others have found annoying and have never taken an action to resolve.

As you proceed through this section, keep in mind that the college survival course as an isolated entity probably will not significantly increase retention rates. It will, however, enhance a comprehensive retention program. Remember that the lack of a sense of connection to the institution often contributes heavily to students' failure to continue with their studies. This sense of estrangement can be especially prevalent in the groups of students considered in this section. The nature and design of the college survival course can foster a feeling of inclusion among students. Adding specific academic and life skills to this feeling of belonging will only strengthen your students' ability and determination to persevere.

Classroom and School Strategies

College survival is a function of activities taking place at many different locations within a school and involves every teacher, administrator, and staff person. This section offers strategies for improving student retention inside and outside the classroom.

The problem of students dropping out is too big to be solved merely by teaching a college survival course. Many educators believe that presenting a course on how to be successful in school is the single most effective strategy for decreasing dropouts. And all agree that more can be done. The problem is significant.

The following suggestions come from a series of workshops presented by Dave Ellis over the last several years to thousands of educators in the United States and Canada. The procedures outlined next are a condensation of his lectures. If you would like more information on any of these ideas, please call College Survival at 800-528-8323.

As suggested to students in *Becoming a Master Student*, use only what works for you. Look through this list of student retention ideas. Some of the following suggestions will be senseless for your school. Many of them might already have been implemented. Check what you can implement, then devise a plan to bring it about.

Own it all—"But it's not my job. I know that somebody ought to do it, but that's not why I was hired. And besides, if I did try to do something about it, I would probably just make someone mad." Yes, that might be true. Change can be upsetting. The suggestion is to do what you see needs doing, even if it is not your job—even if someone might get mad. Look around, see what needs to happen to promote college survival at your school, and then make it your job to see that it happens. If you "own it all," that doesn't mean you have to do it all. It just suggests that you make sure somebody does.

Look around the room in which you spend most of your work time. Look around the institution as a whole and ask yourself: What needs to be done? When you come up with several answers, pick one. Develop a plan for getting it done and then put your plan into action. Break out of the mold of tunnel vision. Walk around as if you own the place and act accordingly.

Recognize student priorities—Our natural tendency is to assume that students are as interested as we are in the subjects we teach. "Surely students understand and appreciate the importance of what I teach." They don't always.

Most students have priorities far different from those that educators usually recognize. Far ahead of the class material, students' priorities include grades, graduation, part-time jobs, children, money, relationships (spouses, friends, lovers), sports, purchases, and on and on. As educators, if we recognize this priority structure, it is much easier to provide relevant incentives for effective student behavior. If you want students to devote time and energy to course material, you usually have to provide a consequence

  Copyright © Houghton Mifflin Company. All rights reserved.

for the assignment (quiz, discussion, report). Even with some of the most motivated students, it just doesn't work to say, "For tomorrow, I would like you to read all of Chapter Seven. It is not anything you will be tested on, and it is not critical to the rest of the material in this class, but it is very interesting. I'm sure you will enjoy it."

The attitude of some teachers seems to be "Well, too bad. If students are going to learn only material that they will use in the next class or sometime soon, or if they will learn only that upon which they will be tested, or if they are only interested in what is immediately relevant, too bad." Too bad for the student and for the teacher. Student priorities are not what we often wish they would be. We can either ignore the fact or we can assist students to grow by recognizing and working within their priorities.

Provide tutoring—A modest amount of individual assistance is often just what is needed to get a student from a position of "I'm completely lost" to "Oh, I get it now!" Tutoring can come from several sources, even when budgets are tight.

Peer tutors are often the answer. Students will usually tutor other students at a very low cost to the institution. This can be set up through a student service center, counseling department, dean's office, or the library. It is possible at most schools to offer student tutors credit (maybe just transcript credit that does not apply toward graduation) in addition to money, or even in lieu of money. High-achieving students are often sensitive to the opinions of future employers. Students recognize the credibility demonstrated when an interviewer sees a résumé or transcript showing good grades and also the ability to tutor others.

Tutoring can also be handled by full-time professional tutors or as an adjunct responsibility for faculty members. Tutoring provides an alternative to large group or traditional classroom instruction, neither of which works well for some students.

Examine the registration process—A common theme on college campuses seems to be "Wow, you should see our freshman registration. What a zoo! If a student can make it through that experience, he is bound to be persistent enough to graduate." There also seems to be a fatalistic attitude that implies that nothing can be done about it.

Many colleges have effectively computerized and/or decentralized the registration process and thereby removed long lines, increased student scheduling options, and humanized an often robot-like interchange between students and advisors.

Registration is often the students' first impression of your school. First impressions are lasting.

Realize that commitment is not enough—Educators often accuse failing students of not being motivated. Evidence seems to suggest otherwise. Students are motivated to succeed. Students generally start college by telling everyone they know. It is a big deal. They announce to friends, family members, and the guy at the corner store that they are "off to college." Students are aware of the costs. If you are not convinced of that, listen to the complaining when they pay for books or tuition. They also know the benefits of an education. (Most of them didn't enroll for the fun of going to class.) Students have a great deal invested in success.

For some students, going to school represents a last chance for breaking a failing pattern. They have high hopes as they begin their education. They are motivated. Motivation or commitment is often not enough. Flying at an altitude of 30,000 feet in a Boeing 747 can be frightening if the pilot and copilot suddenly disappear. No matter how much motivation you have, you are not likely to learn how to fly in time to safely land the plane.

To learn a complex new skill, we need to learn one small piece at a time. By blaming failure on lack of motivation, we too easily ignore a road to success—divide and conquer. Almost any student can learn highly complex material if it is presented in small pieces and if mastery of each piece is gained before moving forward.

What appears to be a lack of commitment is usually an avoidance of continuing failure. Most of us quit and become "unmotivated" after repeated failure and little or no experience of success. The solution to this dilemma is to build on success. Jon Carlson, when interviewed by Bob Edwards on National

Copyright © Houghton Mifflin Company. All rights reserved.

Public Radio, told this story. A little girl came to him one day and said, "Dr. Carlson, Dr. Carlson, look at my paper." She then showed him a paper upon which every word was spelled wrong. He said, "Maureen, I really like your paper. The margins are nice and neat, and your printing is clean and readable." She replied, "Thank you, Dr. Carlson. I've really been working hard on it. Next I'm going to work on my spelling."

Identify potential dropouts—Labeling or categorizing can often lead to a self-fulfilling prophecy. It can also be a useful tool in determining where to place valuable resources.

When you identify students who are likely to drop out, you create an opportunity to promote them in ways that might not be necessary for all students. They might get special tutoring, reduced schedules, remedial classes, extra encouragement, or supplemental learning material.

Research studies proliferate on the most reliable way to predict potential dropouts. Suggestions include looking at high school grades, college entrance test scores, socioeconomic indices, and even personality characteristics. Many researchers agree that the simplest and most effective predictor of students who will drop out is first-term grades. Those students who fail one or more classes during the first term of college are most likely to drop out before completing their education.

While failure might not cause more failure, it does predict it well.

Make counseling available—No matter what the budgetary constraints of your institution, you can make counseling available to students. If it is not possible to have a trained and certified personal counselor at your school, you can still make one available to students. Establish a referral arrangement with a local counseling agency.

Communities of almost every size have public or church-funded counseling agencies that will set up a referral system with you. You will then have a direct and easy path for students to get help in coping with problems of divorce, death, alcoholism, children, stress, and so on. Some counseling agencies work on a sliding fee scale, so money does not have to be a barrier to getting help.

Perform a climate check—Often we don't know what is going on with students. It is easy to assume the best or the worst. Check it out. Find out what is going on with students at your school. You can assess student opinion formally with a written survey or informally with "Psst, hey, what do you think of this place anyway?"

Schedule faculty hours—A frequent complaint of students seems to be "I know I should go see the teacher, but I can never find him." When students are reminded that their teacher has office hours from 2 to 4 p.m. on Tuesday and Thursday, they often retort, "Yeah, well, I went to see him during those hours two different times, and he was never there." What the student doesn't know is that one of these times the teacher had a faculty meeting and the other time he was just down the hall getting a cup of coffee.

Students are usually reluctant to approach teachers outside of class. Once they do get up the courage to come and see a teacher, it is important that he be available. Include at least one visit with the instructor as part of the grade for this course. Consider setting aside an hour or two a week when students know that, without fail, the teacher can be easily located. The excuse "He's never around" is thereby eliminated.

Tour the school as a student. It is easy to miss seeing how your school looks through the eyes of a student. The routine of our day-to-day work can slowly blind us to the realities of our institutions. Once every week or two, put on your "student glasses" and walk around the school. Look at the buildings, look at the walls, floors, and bulletin boards as if you were a student. Read announcements from the perspective of a student. Sit in the business office or the financial aid office and wait for an appointment. Look at the faces of the people behind the desks. Ask yourself what it might look like and how it might feel to a student.

Glance in open classroom doors. Better yet, sit in a classroom for an entire class, not for just a few minutes. Imagine yourself as a student; then make a list of all that could be changed so that students would more likely be successful. Take on two or three of the items on your list as projects to accomplish. Keep a journal about your experiences and observations, and share parts of your journal in class.

   Copyright © Houghton Mifflin Company. All rights reserved.

Videotape yourself as you teach—This is one of the most effective faculty development tools around. The taping can be done by a student or a staff person from the school's media resource center. The viewing is best done privately. Supervisors can add so much additional tension to the viewing that personal insights are almost impossible.

Seeing yourself on videotape can be unsettling. Most of us are shocked the first time we hear our voices on a tape recorder. That experience is magnified when sight and sound are combined. One way to get value from the viewing is to set up a VCR, a TV, the tape of your class, and a box of tissues in a private room. Then take notes.

When viewing the videotape, be certain to record as many compliments as suggestions. Our tendency is to see with a critical eye only. Balance that with a commitment to write at least as many positive evaluations as negative ones.

Concentrate efforts on first-term students—Student retention research indicates that by far the largest concentration of students leaving school is during and right after the first quarter or semester. This is the most effective time in the student's career to provide additional support.

Look around to see what can be done to ensure the success of first-term students. What is needed? An extended orientation course as described in this Course Manual is certainly one way to provide extra assistance to first-term students. Improving the quality of instruction for first-term students is another option.

It is typical in colleges to assign more experienced instructors to upper-division classes. As a reward for experience and excellence, teachers are given the students who have been in college the longest. This might be a nice reward for teachers; however, from the standpoint of college survival, the policy is ineffective. New students, more than any others, need the most experienced teachers. Consider having those teachers who know how best to capture student attention be the teachers who work with first-term students.

Orient parents and spouses—Let a student's spouse or parents know what is available at the school. Develop a short orientation program so that the significant people in students' lives can have a direct experience of the institution that is going to be demanding so much of their time, money, and energy.

This is an opportunity to "sell" the whole family, the student's primary support group, on the value of the college experience. If they are sold, they are much more likely to be supportive of the long hours and hard work required to be successful in school.

Use alumni—Financial contributions are all that is usually requested of past graduates. They can offer much more. Consider using them as department advisors, career consultants, or guest speakers.

As department advisors, they can meet once every few months with the head of the department, a few faculty, and other alumni to discuss proposed departmental changes, curriculum additions or modifications, placement strategies, or new directions in the field.

Alumni can act as career consultants by working through the placement department and by being willing to talk to students who are exploring career options. In addition to standard career consulting techniques, students can often gain tremendous insight by visiting with someone "in the field." This visit is even more relevant when the professional is a graduate of the school the student is attending. It is best if the student can visit the alumnus's workplace.

As guest speakers, alumni can add timeliness and credibility to almost any message or content presentation. They can certainly add variety. Most people like to teach, and alumni are often willing to donate time and energy when given a chance to share their expertise.

Continue to "sell" students—This idea is offensive to some administrators and many professors, who consider themselves "above that sort of thing." Selling has gotten a bad name in academic circles, and the idea of viewing students as customers is unacceptable to some. Please use another term if you prefer.

Most of us need to be continually reminded that we are spending our lives on what is important and valuable. We want to know that getting up in the morning, fighting the traffic, and spending the day

Copyright © Houghton Mifflin Company. All rights reserved.

working are not in vain. Students want to know the same thing. Students can be reminded of the value of their "purchase" by teachers in class and by administrators through letters and brochures. As teachers, we can interject brief messages of encouragement and support, such as "Last night when I was reading about ——, I realized again how exciting and worthwhile it is to study," or "I was pleased to find out about the job a former student is doing at such and such a company. He graduated from our department."

Know that "not enough money" is an excuse—While, this is not always true, generally it is the easiest answer to the question "Why are you dropping out?" We are not always aware of our motivations or the reasons behind our behavior. Maybe when a student says he is dropping out because he can't afford it, what he is really saying is "Given what I am getting, it is not worth it." At that point, it is supportive of the student's success in school to ask him what he is getting, or better still, not getting.

After the student knows you have heard his concerns about not having enough money, it is often effective to ask, "If you had enough money, why would you want to drop out?" He is likely to shake his head and state, "I didn't say I would drop out if I had the money." "Well, would you?" you can ask. "Yeah, I think so. I just failed my second accounting test, and I just think I am in the wrong major."

When the first excuse is money, the second reason is often the bottom line. If you can deal with that concern, often the problem of not having enough money can be more easily resolved. The student might do more part-time work, borrow money from someone in the family, sell something, postpone buying something, or discover a new source of financial aid.

Often, as in the previous example, the second reason has something to do with failure. Repeated failure, especially in a new environment not associated with many successes, can quickly lead to an avoidance response. When students don't experience at least some success in school, they are likely to leave.

Reward students—Establish rewards for just about anything you can imagine. Set up a rewards ceremony every few months and acknowledge every major and minor accomplishment possible. Pass out plaques, ribbons, certificates, and trophies. Have a special dean's list for part-time students. Award for grades, attendance, skill levels achieved, and so on. Be corny! Surely in this day of sophistication, you might argue, students are not going to accept a sophomoric display or crass reinforcement of positive behavior. Try it. We all love it.

Or don't try it. If you are convinced that students don't need or want this type of corny public acknowledgment and recognition, then skip this idea. Experiment with lots of different strategies for promoting college survival and use what works.

Hold a presidential luncheon lottery—Identify the people on your campus whom students see as the administrative leaders. They might be the president, the chancellor, directors, and deans. Then set up a lottery in which students sign their names and phone numbers on tickets and drop them in a box. Each month, three names are drawn, and those students go to lunch with the president (or the person whom you believe students see as having the most influence at the institution). Make this luncheon a big deal. Everybody gets dressed up and goes to one of the nicest restaurants in town. The school pays.

The advantage of this type of meeting is that it lets students know that their opinions are valued. This is a time for students to talk and for the president to listen. Students can share their concerns and voice their complaints without listening to defensive justifications or worrying about having to "solve" problems. This is not a time for a "state of the university" address. It is simply a time to listen to students. Many administrators do not take the time to be with students. They slowly lose touch with what is happening in the lives of students. This is a monthly chance to find out what is needed and wanted by the people we are dedicated to serve.

Have a "donuts with a dean" program—Design a structure for inviting students to have donuts with a dean. Use a lottery, ask teachers to recommend students, send random invitations, or have contests. This variation of the presidential luncheon lottery allows more administrators to have more direct contact with more students. This idea can be modified to facilitate students having donuts with their teachers as well.

   Copyright © Houghton Mifflin Company. All rights reserved.

Establish student internships and externships—Provide a work experience for each student sometime before he graduates. This can be a simulated work environment set up by the school or a part-time temporary placement with a local employer. It is usually possible to find employers who will provide some training in exchange for free labor.

This internship or externship will provide students with a chance to experience directly the type of work they will be doing when they graduate. This can tie together work they have done in courses that might have seemed unrelated or irrelevant.

Use several approaches—It is difficult to predict just what change or which new program will have the most impact on college survival. It is possible to spend so much time researching alternatives and looking for the "best" approach that nothing gets done. Experiment with several techniques at once. Several combined approaches will often be just what is needed.

Put the most capable person in charge—At most schools, there is no one person responsible for college survival and retention. Often, "everyone is in charge" is the same as "no one is in charge." Find a person at your school who gets things done and put him in charge of improving the student retention rate. Find the most capable person and have him be the one responsible for decreasing student dropout.

Maybe that person is a teacher. Maybe he's an administrator. Maybe he is already working directly with students in a counseling center. Maybe that person is you. Whoever it is, give him a new job. Assign the job of improving student retention to one person. He can then get help from others in your school.

The person in charge of improving student retention can start by reviewing the ideas in this list and in other books written on student retention and establishing an action plan. The results of the plan can be monitored and measured, then revisions can be made to the plan. Through experimentation you will find what works at your school.

Train tutors—Student tutors and professional tutors alike need to be taught or reminded how to effectively encourage students to be academically successful. Set up a monthly meeting of all tutors and review basic teaching techniques and specific methods for being an effective tutor.

Faculty members from departments of education and outstanding teachers from any department of your school can be guest speakers at monthly tutor-training meetings. Also, frank and open discussions about the frustrations and successes of tutors can be valuable training.

Provide a midpoint reward—Halfway through their programs, provide each student with some type of recognition. This could be a certificate, a ceremony, a pin, a dinner, or any gesture that acknowledges their making it halfway.

There is a business school in the Northeast that teaches an airline and travel course. As a midpoint reward, it takes the students on a cruise to the Bahamas. The transportation costs are paid by the school. Of course, overall tuition was raised to pay for the cost of the trip. In the long run, the school gains by a decrease in the dropout rate. This generous reward will not be possible at most schools. Stretch your imagination to find an appropriate way to congratulate students for completing half of their journey toward graduation.

Adopt a student—Look around and see who needs some special attention. Find a student whom you like and who you think needs extra encouragement. Adopt that student. Do what you can to ensure the success of that one person. This suggestion is sometimes criticized. People say that it is showing favoritism and partiality and seems to be suggesting that students should not all be treated the same. They are right—it is.

Confess areas of ineffectiveness—At least once a month, sit down with paper and pencil and take an honest inventory of your professional behavior. Look for what doesn't work in how you do your job. Consider the specific ways that you are ineffective.

Copyright © Houghton Mifflin Company. All rights reserved.

Write them down. Take the time to closely examine what you do that doesn't work. Look for things you have done recently that have not promoted college survival. Consider what you could change to improve the quality of your work.

This suggestion is not counter to positive thinking. It is great to have a positive self-image and to remind ourselves frequently of what we have done well. Nevertheless, it is also necessary to know what we have done that is not effective so that we can have an opportunity to change.

Look through the eyes of the nontraditional student—As demographic studies indicate, the average age of students is increasing. Students who return to school after several years often experience education differently. These students might have been homemakers, laborers, business operators, service men or women, world travelers, or hermits. They are likely to see things differently than a student fresh out of high school.

Take time to imagine how your school appears to the nontraditional student. Are the rules appropriate? Do lecture examples include older students? Is the atmosphere of student lounge facilities inviting and inclusive? Are activities designed to include everyone?

Explain the problems when recruiting. Students often approach school with unrealistic expectations. They might expect all the buildings to have tall columns and ivy. They might think their new instructors will be better than any they have ever had. They often imagine they will be attending Shangri-La U.

There are two distinct advantages to explaining problems when you recruit students. First, it brings expectations more in line with reality. Second, it raises the credibility of the person who is recruiting for the school.

Often people who recruit new students are seen strictly as salespeople. Their credibility might be questioned because it is their job to increase student enrollment. When they point out potential problems and the possible deficiencies of the school, they present a balanced report and possibly spare the student adjustment problems later on.

Realize that some students are better off leaving—Help them pack their bags. Not all students are meant to graduate. Their life goals might be best reached by leaving school. If this is the case, help them out. Really help them out.

Keep in mind that student retention improves when we promote college survival. Sometimes, this means encouraging the student to stay in school even though it is very hard work, demanding personal sacrifice. Sometimes we might recommend leaving school.

Use exit interviews—Exit interviews can be conducted in person, by telephone, or through surveys. The key is to find out why students leave school. Many students do not officially drop out. They sort of fade away. At some point you know they are gone, and there was no time when they actually reported to a school official that they were leaving. In that case, the exit interview is more difficult to conduct, and it shouldn't be ignored. Exit interviews can be done over the phone with students who do not officially drop out. For those who cannot be reached by phone, a letter and a short questionnaire can provide the data.

The purpose of the exit interview is to find patterns in the many reasons why students drop out. A personal interview is the most effective way to gather this information. However, it will not work well if it is seen by the student as a way to talk him out of his decision to leave.

Collect precise data and post it—Many administrators do not know the exact data on their student retention rate. They know it is not what they want it to be, and they might even know approximately what it is. The strength of data comes from quantity and precision.

Each term, compute the retention rate of new and returning students. Compare this with precise figures from previous terms. Look for trends in programs, in types of students, and in the time of year.

Do a "by name" assessment. Knowing the number of students enrolled at the beginning of one term and the number enrolled at the beginning of the following term does not distinguish between predicted attrition and natural attrition. Predicted attrition involves students who have expressed their intention to

   Copyright © Houghton Mifflin Company. All rights reserved.

leave after one term and might not indicate any problems that can be corrected. Raw numbers from one term to the next do not account for late arrivals who enroll after the term begins. Also, these numbers do not compare the retention rates of students who have taken a college survival course with those who have not. Knowing the precise attributes of students who have been retained and those who have not can suggest specific strategies to improve retention.

Make this data available to those people who have the most influence on college survival. They can look for more effective ways to promote college survival and can celebrate improvements in retention rates.

Forget about improving retention. Concentrate on improving college survival. Dropout rates will consequently decrease.

Set up a prepayment program—Allow students to make advance payments on the anticipated difference between their financial aid award and the cost of their education. If for some reason the student did not start classes, this prepayment would be refunded with interest accrued.

The advantage of this system goes beyond encouraging wise budgeting. A prepayment is a form of commitment. It demonstrates in one more way a student's determination to start or to continue his education.

Use flextime for student problem solving. It is difficult for some students to complete their financial aid forms, pay their bills, register for their classes, pick up their test papers, or meet with their instructors between 8 a.m. and 5 p.m. It might serve students' needs if some offices were open for extended weekday hours and on Saturday mornings.

Recruit graduates—Rather than recruiting freshmen who might drop out, admissions personnel can recruit students who are likely to graduate. Entrance examinations can be used to help students decide if they have a reasonable chance of being successful in your school.

Academically underprepared students and students with career interests not served by your school are unlikely to become graduates. Consider discouraging their enrollment.

Establish developmental programs—For those students who are academically underprepared, provide a way for them to strengthen their skills. It is possible to significantly improve basic reading, writing, and mathematics skills in a short time. Set up classes or individual learning experiences in which students can prepare themselves academically.

Basic math and English courses are available as elective courses, required courses, or independent, self-paced study programs. These are often competency based, so students' progress can be monitored and a level of performance required before they are allowed to register for the next term. Small classes with specially trained instructors generally have excellent results in increasing basic skills. Students are then prepared to be successful.

Intervene—This notion is foreign to many educators who grew up with the philosophy to "live and let live." It seems somehow old-fashioned and even inappropriate to get involved in another person's life. Consider doing it anyway.

When students begin their post-secondary education, they do it out of choice. They select a school on the basis of many factors, including where they think they can be successful. In a real sense, they buy that chance for success with their tuition dollars. They are entering into a contract that says, "If I do this . . . , I will get this. . . ." They expect to graduate and to receive all of the benefits associated with graduating. And they expect to do what is required to get to graduation. Often we don't tell them what is required. We don't want to meddle, to intrude, to interfere.

To intervene is appropriate when you have been given permission. By their choice to pursue graduating from your school, students have given that permission. They have, in a sense, said, "Tell me periodically how I am doing in my quest for graduation." It therefore seems appropriate to report what you see.

This reporting might even include the following approaches. In a telephone call to the home of a student, you might say, "I am concerned about your attendance. Your absence today was the fourth this

Copyright © Houghton Mifflin Company. All rights reserved.

term." After a class, you might tell the student, "I wonder if you're having a difficult time sticking with what is happening in class. It looks like your attention is seldom on the lecture or the class discussion." In a letter, you might write, "Please call me or see me after class and make an appointment to discuss your progress. I want you to be successful."

Set up an emergency loan fund—"For the want of a nail the war was lost." Sometimes a few dollars are all that is needed to survive a financial crisis. A twenty-dollar loan might solve the current emergency and prevent a more drastic solution, such as dropping out to get a job.

In times of financial stress, it is difficult to keep long-term goals firmly in mind. Priorities seem to rearrange themselves, and getting a few dollars becomes all important. An emergency loan fund can be a temporary solution to short-term financial problems.

This emergency loan would have low interest, a modest limit ($30 to $80), and a short term (two to four months). The loan could be processed quickly and the money disbursed within minutes of application. At some schools, this type of loan has been financed by student contributions and fundraisers.

Challenge students—Boredom can be tolerated if it is not pervasive. Students will generally put up with a lot of tedium if they have one thing that is challenging. Provide some opportunity for stretching. Academic adventure can be provided by extraordinary class projects, unusual assignments, outside readings that allow for creativity, or substitute classes. Even one independent study class or project within a class can be an avenue for academic challenge.

Invert the curriculum—The traditional college curriculum postpones "major" courses until the second or third year of study. A freshman excited about psychology is likely to get his first "real" course only after several semesters of general education. Inverting the curriculum would allow the student to begin his study of psychology first thing.

This same approach can be applied in each class. Material that students consider the "real thing" can be presented up front. Foundations do need to be laid, and this can be done along with the material that students consider to be the "meat" of the course. In a computer course, students can be taught to write a computer program on the first day. In an accounting course, a simple financial statement for a well-known business can be reviewed immediately. In a chemistry course, an experiment can be performed by each student during the first week.

Institute a retention bonus—Consider paying staff and faculty a year-end bonus based on a decrease in the student dropout rate. Profit in proprietary schools is almost a direct function of student retention rates. Revenue in private schools is directly affected by student retention. Even many public institutions are immediately affected by student dropouts. A retention bonus assumes that employees of the school have a direct effect on student retention and that people are motivated by money.

A bonus to all employees need not be evenly distributed. Those people who have the most direct student contact could be eligible for a larger bonus. All bonuses would be dependent on the school's meeting a predetermined improvement in the retention rate, and further improvements might even raise the amount of the bonus. For example, if the retention rate of first-term students improved by at least 5 percent of the average retention rate of the previous three years, then each instructor teaching first-term students would receive a $400 bonus, and all other teachers and employees would receive $200.

(CAUTION: As with all suggestions, this one abounds with potential—potential benefits and potential trouble. Standards have to be maintained. Fairness is always questioned. Educators do not like to be seen as mercenary. And money is an excellent motivator that often gets people to discover new and effective ways to promote college survival.)

Examine attitudes at financial aid and business offices—Unknowingly, people who work with students and money can fall into a pattern of being patronizing and condescending. Awareness is the key to change.

   Copyright © Houghton Mifflin Company. All rights reserved.

Develop in-service for faculty to set the stage for faculty development—This can include daylong workshops with outside presenters or monthly meetings in which discussion centers on how classes can be conducted more effectively. The material presented does not have to be new and innovative to be effective. Often we just need to be reminded to continue to use that which we know works.

A useful format for faculty development is one in which teachers are encouraged to brainstorm suggestions for improving classroom instruction, student services, and administrative operations and policies. These brainstorms, occurring at the beginning of each meeting, can get energy flowing and set the stage for useful discussion. Remember that the purpose of the brainstorm is quantity, not quality, and outrageous ideas often lead to the discovery of the best suggestions.

Brainstormed lists can be typed and distributed for future discussion and evaluation. Evaluation of brainstorms is most effective when done with selection as a goal rather than deletion. That is, time can be spent selecting items to be expanded or implemented, rather than spending time deleting those items that are considered ridiculous or unworkable.

Use student representatives on committees—It is generally easier to accept policies and decisions that we have a hand in making. Students generally take committee assignments very seriously. An alternative to this might be to set up a president's advisory board composed of students.

Examine housing conditions—Look at where students are living. This might include campus housing or local apartment complexes. If housing conditions are not conducive to success, discuss with students the impact of living environments on success. Search for alternatives and help them improve their housing conditions.

Get a commitment to return after breaks—Look for ways to get students to indicate their intention to return to school after each break. Over vacations and between terms are likely times for students to decide to drop out of school. You can get some idea that this might occur if students are reluctant to share their plans about the future.

Ways to get some type of commitment include preregistration, course project preliminary plans (have students submit an outline of what their class projects will involve), prepayment of tuition or fees, and surveys. Informally, this commitment can be requested verbally—"Is everything set for you for next term?"

Make helpers highly visible—Students who need assistance might not be aggressive in looking for help. Advisors, counselors, tutors, financial aid officers, and other student services personnel can be made visible by office location, bulletin board advertisements, brochures, and frequent class announcements promoting student services.

Set up a summer (prestart) orientation program—Sometime before classes actually start, reach every student on campus. Personal contact with school personnel and the facilities will increase the chances that the student starts class and is successful.

Provide day care—As the number of older students starting school increases, the needs of the student body change. Finding competent and trusted care for children is an activity that occupies hours of many students' lives. It is possible to provide day care without actually operating a center.

Locate a day care center close to school and set up a referral program. Some centers will provide discounts for members of certain groups, such as students attending your school.

Individualize instruction—It might not be practical to allow students to progress at their own rate in every class they take. It is desirable to allow self-directed and self-paced instruction in at least some part of at least one class every term. Most students want the independence of choosing their own direction.

Individualized instruction provides a way for students to feel some autonomy and to take responsibility for some aspect of their education. It gives the student who does not function well in a rigid system a chance to set his own pace. Advanced students can have the experience of racing forward, and underachieving students can move at a pace that allows them to master the material.

Copyright © Houghton Mifflin Company. All rights reserved.

Review policies and rules—Students report that meaningless rules and regulations are one of their greatest frustrations and a frequent reason that they drop out of school. It might not be possible to change all of the rules that students find objectionable, yet it is possible to modify policies and rules that no longer make sense.

We are habitual animals, and our institutions model our rigidity. There might be dozens of rules and regulations at your school that could be changed with no harm done to the purposes and goals of your institution. A policy that made perfect sense when it was developed fifty years ago might now need to be changed.

Ask students what doesn't make sense and then see what you can change. When you are asking for student opinion, make it clear that you cannot follow all of their suggestions. Stress that you will do all you can to accommodate their needs.

Set up an advocacy program—Consider assigning one advocate or advisor to every group of 10 to 15 students. These advocates can be faculty members, staff, or administrators. Their purpose would be to meet with the group of students and identify ways in which they could help the students achieve their goals.

These group meetings would begin immediately after the start of school and would be scheduled at least once a month during the first term and less frequently thereafter. During the meetings, students would get a chance to meet several other students, talk about goals, make suggestions, discuss frustrations and accomplishments, ask questions, and receive specific tips on adjusting to a new environment.

Encourage regular attendance at the meetings and follow up on each student who does not attend. Specific problems and suggestions can be communicated by the advocate to the appropriate school personnel.

Establish extracurricular activities—Even the smallest school can have a program of extracurricular activities. Having a football team or a symphony orchestra is not the only way to get students involved with each other outside of the classroom. A bowling club or barbershop quartet can accomplish the same thing. Set up some way for students to become involved with the school and with other students outside of academics.

Write or update an advisory handbook—The people at your school who advise students often learn by legend. They pass on to students what has been passed on to them. What they advise might be wrong, even though a lot of people believe it. Constructing or revising a handbook might lead to clarification of policies and rules that have become mysteries.

Select advisors carefully—Not all teachers are suited to advise students. A person might interact very well with a group of students and not interact well in one-on-one situations. Selection is most effective when it starts with self-selection. People often know when they wouldn't do an effective job. And others will say that they just don't want to. It is unlikely that you would want people who don't like that type of work to be advising.

Solicit schoolwide support—Ask everyone to be involved in the job of promoting college survival. It is possible to just clean the classrooms, and it is possible to clean the classrooms with the idea of promoting college survival. The job is done differently in subtle and significant ways.

When we do our work with the purpose of helping students, we usually find ways that we can do the job more effectively. (Working efficiently is doing a job right; working effectively is doing the *right* job right.) Every teacher, administrator, and staff member can have an impact on college survival every day.

Schedule a Faculty and Staff Appreciation Day—Form a committee composed of administrators, faculty, staff, and students to plan a special day to honor the faculty and staff. Fun and food can be combined with sincere expressions of gratitude. Perhaps the student government would like to be responsible for this event.

    Copyright © Houghton Mifflin Company. All rights reserved.

Schedule a Student Appreciation Day—Form a committee to plan a special day to honor students. Improved morale contributes to improved retention rates. Administrators, faculty, and staff can be creative and brainstorm a long list of ways to demonstrate their appreciation of students.

Ask others to get involved—Set up a task force on college survival that cuts across all areas of the college. Post the purpose of "serve students" in prominent places as a reminder for all to see. Send letters internally reporting on what is being done specifically to promote college survival and asking for ideas. Get everyone involved.

Establish a required, ongoing orientation program—College Survival is available to help schools implement continuing orientation classes. This type of course would meet at least once a week for a minimum of 30 contact hours and would be required of all full-time, nontransfer students as a for-credit course. The course covers study skills and life skills appropriate for being successful in school, and it encourages the use of school and community resources.

Assume the validity of the Power Process "I create it all." Consider for a moment the ridiculous notion that you are responsible for every student who drops out of school. Then look for ways that you create those dropouts. By using this idea, you might discover strategies for promoting college survival that you never would have otherwise considered.

Support warmth, friendliness, and caring—An environment of love is apparent, even though it cannot easily be defined. People can feel when they are in a place that is friendly, warm, and caring. The way to effect this change is simple and requires lots of energy. Commit to the change and talk it up. In every interaction and in every conversation, each of us can communicate our warmth, friendliness, and caring. It soon becomes contagious.

The Role of Faculty

Stressing the benefits of staying in school is an essential part of eliciting support for your course. Depending on course content, following are some of the benefits students can expect:

- Difficult tasks, assignments, and papers take less time.
- Learning obstacles disappear.
- Employability is enhanced.
- Investment in education is more likely to pay off.
- School is more enjoyable.
- Grades improve.
- Studying is more productive.
- Academic, career, and life goals are in focus.
- Anxiety level is reduced.
- More hours are available for fun, work, study, or sleep.
- Notes are legible and useful.
- Inquiry skills improve.
- Tests are approached more confidently and skillfully.
- Stressful situations are easier to handle.
- Choice of school or major is clarified.
- Policies and rules that govern the institution are understood.
- Communication skills improve.
- Support groups are established.
- Self-confidence increases.
- Involvement in the educational community increases.
- Procrastination diminishes.

Copyright © Houghton Mifflin Company. All rights reserved.

- Relationships improve with spouses, teachers, roommates, friends, parents, children, and so on.
- Money is managed better.
- Campus and community resources become more familiar.
- Endorsement by the faculty is critical to the foundation of your college survival course.

Faculty support can include the following steps:

- Promote the academic credibility of your course, recognize its creditworthiness, and take appropriate action, if necessary, in the faculty senate or curriculum committee in order to get the course approved.
- Provide feedback to college survival course instructors about student needs and/or deficiencies. Later, faculty can provide information about how your course is influencing student behavior.
- Speak positively about your course to students, parents, administrators, and fellow faculty members.
- Take part in a retention task force or orientation committee.
- Be directly involved through teaching, team teaching, or facilitating one or more sections.
- Participate in your course as a guest speaker.
- Reinforce concepts and methods introduced in the college survival course and incorporate them into individual disciplines.
- Refer students to your course (if the course isn't mandatory).

Here are some course benefits that might be of interest to the faculty:

- Teaching is more productive and enjoyable. Students are awake, active, responsible for their learning, and task oriented. Students learn to teach themselves.
- Students who acquire lifelong learning skills have a greater appreciation for education and for the teachers who provide an opportunity for learning.
- Improved retention results in greater revenue and high student numbers. These in turn can increase demand for faculty, create support to improve facilities, and, in terms of budget cuts, enhance the security of teaching positions.
- College survival courses provide an unusual opportunity to interact with students on a personal level.
- More upper-division classes are available to teach due to the increased number of upper class students.
- Faculty members who teach this type of course enjoy additional benefits. Being a part of the exciting discoveries students make and observing changes in student attitudes can renew one's sense of what is possible in education.

The Role of Administrators

Administrators provide key elements in support of college survival courses. Ask them to contribute to the success of the course in such ways as the following:

- Recognizing the potential of your course and including it as an essential part of the institutional retention plan
- Promoting the activity of a retention task force or committee. This can include scheduling and announcing meetings, requesting members to participate actively and perform specific tasks, and setting timelines.
- Ensuring that your course carries academic credit if that is within administrative control. College survival courses can be a viable part of a core curriculum. In many instances, they fulfill general education requirements.
- Making your course mandatory for all new students, if appropriate

   Copyright © Houghton Mifflin Company. All rights reserved.

- Listing your course in the catalog and enrollment documents as a legitimate part of the curriculum
- Scheduling your course in attractive time slots
- Taking responsibility for the details of registration. It is common for a newly required college survival course to falter at registration if some workers are unaware that scheduling each student into the course is mandatory.
- Ensuring that rooms and equipment are available and adequate
- Participating as guest speakers
- Teaching or facilitating one or more sections. Although this might go beyond the typical show of support, it would be a substantial demonstration of the administration's belief in the importance of your course. Presidents, vice presidents, and deans often make excellent teachers of a college survival course. Participating in this way can also enhance their relationships with students.
- Publicly voicing their support of your course to students, faculty, and other administrators
- Selecting instructors who care about college survival. Ideally, teachers will give students an opportunity to experiment with new methods and techniques rather than merely lecturing about them.

When asking for these and other measures of support from administrators, emphasize course benefits that will affect them specifically, such as the following:

- Enhanced student performance as measured by grade point averages, number of courses completed per term per student, and persistence to graduation
- Stronger financial position of the department and institution due to a higher number of paying customers. Most schools spend heavily on recruiting and matriculating new students. When these students leave before graduating, they must be replaced, again at high cost. Cutting attrition simultaneously cuts revenue losses.
- More satisfied clients, making it easier to recruit new students. Successful students have positive things to say about your school in their circle of influence. When they graduate and are employed, they can act as models and recruiters for your institution.
- Improved student feedback. A college survival course can provide a new channel for communication between students and the administrators.
- More satisfied faculty. Teaching students who take responsibility for their learning can decrease faculty frustration and complaints. Students bring new learning skills to their other classes and might incidentally help their instructors become more effective. Your course will stimulate new conversations among faculty about teaching and learning.

The following are additional benefits:

- Enhanced faculty awareness about retention
- Reduced need for crisis counseling. Your course can head off little problems before they turn into exit interviews.
- High visibility and more effective use of career counselors, tutors, substance abuse programs, and other campus resources
- A new marketing tool for recruiting. The existence of a college survival course is evidence of your institution's commitment to the success of its students. It can also be used as a way to ease a prospective student's anxiety about his academic skills and ability to cope with college pressures. Inform your admissions staff of the benefits of your college survival course. Consider providing a copy of your course textbook to each admissions representative. Knowing the benefits and having a copy of the textbook to show to students can make her job easier.

Copyright © Houghton Mifflin Company. All rights reserved.

PART V:
ASSESSMENT AND OUTCOMES

Introduction

For nearly everybody, assessment is a part of life. In institutions of higher learning, it is a basic tenet. We assess ourselves. (Did that class session work? Is there a better way to present that material? Even a look in the mirror before leaving the house is a form of self-assessment.) We assess others. (We evaluate student performance on tests, assignments, and exercises. We give grades. We might even serve on committees that determine tenure, promotion, or compensation.) Likewise, others (the department chair or program coordinator, the dean, the students) assess us. A little intimidating, isn't it?

Assessment of the college survival course can have at least three objectives: (1) measurement of levels of student learning, (2) evaluation of individual course sections and/or instructors, and (3) overall assessment of the college survival course as part of a comprehensive retention program. Try viewing assessment as a means to refine your course. Many institutions use uniform assessment instruments or methods. If these do not provide you with sufficient information applicable to your college survival course, consider employing some of the research instruments included in this section to supplement your assessment process. Whether you are a new or a veteran instructor, you might find the information on assessing student learning especially helpful as you modify your course throughout the term.

Course Rationale

The methods you use and the questions you ask to measure outcomes are determined by the purpose of your evaluation. Evaluating course effectiveness helps you discover specific ways to improve the course and provides a rationale for its continuation and expansion.

Evaluations can highlight improvements that will help your course meet its objectives. Teacher effectiveness, selection of content, skills application, and methods of instruction can all be evaluated and improved. Ongoing evaluations can help you make continual adjustments, fine-tune the content, and improve your teaching strategies. Following are some areas you might want to investigate to help you refine the purpose of your course and improve it.

Students
- Does the course meet students' needs?
- Do students take responsibility for their own education?
- Are students able to transfer skills to other classes?
- Are students learning to be active, independent thinkers?
- Do students gain greater confidence in their learning ability?
- Is the course interactive?
- Are students given a voice in what is presented in class?

Instructors
- Do instructors vary their methods to teach to all learning styles?
- Do instructors assess which teaching methods worked well and which didn't?
- Do instructors communicate effectively?
- Are instructors ambitious about the course?

   Copyright © Houghton Mifflin Company. All rights reserved.

- Do instructors invite and facilitate student participation?
- Are instructors following the seven-part course structure?
- Do students participate actively in conversations and sharing?
- Are instructors limiting their lecture time?
- Are students asked to make commitments?
- Are students being held accountable to their commitments?
- Do instructors demonstrate how students can transfer skills?
- Are students encouraged to give honest feedback?

Content

- How could the course be changed to make it more effective?
- Which topics were well received by students and which were not?
- Which guest speakers elicited positive responses from students?
- Are appropriate guest speakers invited to the class?
- Is the faculty being consulted about what to include in the course?
- Is the course flexible enough to respond to student needs?
- Can your upper class students or alumni provide insight into course improvements?

Course Continuation and Expansion

Administrators are more willing to continue a course and even expand it when the course meets outlined objectives. Evaluations help administrators make choices. Following are some areas to consider:

- Is adequate credit given for the course?
- Are there sufficient contact hours to achieve course objectives?
- What impact does the course have on the institution's financial position?
- Should additional class sections be offered?
- Will requiring the class of all students increase retention?
- How can the effectiveness of the course be demonstrated?
- Are qualified instructors recruited to teach the course?
- Are the strategies taught being reinforced in other classes?
- Are instructors of other courses noticing behavioral changes in students?
- Are there objections to the course? If so, what are they?
- How can the course benefit recruitment?
- Does the course influence the student counseling load?
- Does the course influence the use of career counselors?
- Does the course influence the use of tutors and other resources?
- Does the course influence the use of the school library?
- What evidence provides justification for a required course?
- What evidence provides justification for an expanded course?
- Is the course scheduled at reasonable time periods?
- What information would be useful for the retention task force or committee?

Outcomes

College survival courses encourage behavioral changes in areas related to being a successful student. Outcomes are results that can be measured. Once you gather the data, there are several ways to analyze and interpret it. You can use matched pair correlations, select students randomly to be in the course, or design longitudinal, split group, or control group studies to compare students who take the class with those who don't. Following are questions to ask when determining outcomes.

Copyright © Houghton Mifflin Company. All rights reserved.

What Are Retention Rates Over Time?
- What are first-term retention rates?
- What are first-, second-, and third-year retention rates?
- What percentage of students graduate or complete their programs?
- How do the retention rates of students who took the course differ from the retention rates of those who didn't?
- How do the graduation rates of students who took the course differ from the graduation rates of those who didn't?
- If the course is now required, how do current retention rates compare with retention rates before it was required?

What Effect Does the Course Have on Grade Point Averages?
- How does the GPA of students who took the course differ from the GPA of those who didn't?
- Do students who take the course improve and maintain their GPAs better than those who don't take the course?

What Is the Course's Impact on the Number of Credits Completed per Term?
- Do students who take the course complete more credits than those who don't?
- Do students who take the course complete a larger percentage of credits attempted than those who don't?

What Is the Course's Impact on Students' Intentions to Stay in School?
- Do students who take the course intend to stay in school longer than those who don't?

How Does the Course Affect Student Participation in School?
- Do students who take the course participate more in school activities (sports, plays, cultural events, social programs, etc.)?
- Do students who take the course participate more in student organizations (government, social and academic clubs, etc.)?
- Do students who take the course take on more leadership roles?

How Does the Course Affect Student Use of School Resources?
- Are students who take the course better informed about school resources?
- Do students who take the course make more appointments with faculty and counselors?
- Do students who take the course visit the library more frequently?
- Do students who take the course use tutors more often?

Methods

There are several methods of determining the effectiveness of the college survival course. The ultimate measures of course effectiveness are improved student performance and increased retention rates. Following are some ideas about how to evaluate your course.

Frequent Content and Process Evaluations
- Ask students to evaluate both the content and process.
- Request feedback from students on regular class quizzes.
- Note improvement in quiz scores as the term progresses.
- Note improvement in test scores in all other courses.

   Copyright © Houghton Mifflin Company. All rights reserved.

- Ask other instructors to attend and evaluate your course.
- Ask for feedback from other instructors about students' performance.
- Ask administrators to attend and evaluate your course.
- Ask students for feedback during conversations and sharing.
- Videotape students in class, observe their reactions, and evaluate the effectiveness of classroom activities.
- Ask students to interview other students and get recommendations.

Evaluations of the Instructor
- Evaluate yourself after each class period.
- Videotape yourself and critique your style and communication.
- Videotape yourself and ask others to critique your presentation.
- Ask other instructors to attend and evaluate your teaching.

Final Evaluations
- Conduct a thorough and anonymous final evaluation.
- Do an in-depth self-evaluation at the end of the term.
- Survey the faculty about student attitudes and performance.
- Compare student pre- and post-course scores on assessment instruments.
- Compare internal and external locus of control scores.
- Interview students on videotape.
- Compare students' perceptions of their progress on the Discovery Wheel from the beginning to the end of the term.
- Interview individual students to discover what they gained and what changes they recommend.

Follow-Up Evaluations
- Do a follow-up evaluation a few months after the course has ended.
- Form a faculty course evaluation committee.
- Form a student course evaluation committee.
- Form a combined student and faculty course evaluation committee.

Examples of Evaluations
On the following pages are examples of a student course evaluation, a teacher evaluation completed by the students, and a master evaluation form.

Student Course Evaluation

Class _____

Date _____

Instructor _____

(Please do not write your name on this paper.)

1. What did you teach yourself while in this class?

2. Would you recommend this course to a friend?

       Yes   No

3. How would you change the course?

4. What did you find most valuable?

5. What did you find least valuable?

6. How many classes did you miss?

       None   1   2   3   more

7. Of the 12 chapters (Concise Edition, 10 chapters), how many did you read?

       All   9–10   5–8   4 or fewer

8. Approximately what percentage of the exercises from the text did you complete?

       100%   75% or more   50% or fewer   fewer than 50%

Copyright © Houghton Mifflin Company. All rights reserved.

Teacher Evaluation

Name _____

Date _____

School name _____

Address _____

Phone _____

1. Please estimate the amount of total time spent: (Circle one item on each line.)

Lectures	more than 75%	50%–75%	25%–50%	less than 25%
Exercises	more than 75%	50%–75%	25%–50%	less than 25%
Guest speakers and videotapes	more than 75%	50%–75%	25%–50%	less than 25%
Conversations and sharing	more than 75%	50%–75%	25%–50%	less than 25%
Quizzes and evaluations	more than 75%	50%–75%	25%–50%	less than 25%
Previews and reviews	more than 75%	50%–75%	25%–50%	less than 25%
Assignments	more than 75%	50%–75%	25%–50%	less than 25%

Did students participate in conversations and sharing time? Please describe type of sharing.

Which parts of your course received the most favorable response?

Which parts of your course received the least favorable response?

What discoveries have you made about your course?

What changes do you intend to make in your course?

Copyright © Houghton Mifflin Company. All rights reserved.

Master Evaluation Form

This form can be used to summarize final student evaluations. You might wish to share the results with your administration.

Instructor's name _____

Course name _____

Date class ended _____

Student Course Evaluation Summary

1. What did you teach yourself while in the class? (most frequent answers)

2. Would you recommend this course to a friend? (totals from Student Course Evaluation)

    _____ Yes _____ No

3. How would you change the course? (most frequent answers)

4. What did you find most valuable? (most frequent answers)

5. What did you find least valuable? (most frequent answers)

6. How many classes did you miss? (number per category)

    _____ None _____ 1 _____ 2 _____ 3 _____ more

7. Of the 12 chapters (Concise Edition, 10 chapters), how many did you read?
   (number per category)

    _____ All _____ 9–10 _____ 5–8 _____ 4 or fewer

Copyright © Houghton Mifflin Company. All rights reserved.

8. Approximately what percentage of the exercises from the text did you complete? (number of students per category)

   _____ 100%   _____ 75%   _____ 50%   _____ Fewer than 50%

9. Additional student comments:

Demographics

1. Is the course required?   Yes   No

2. Is it offered for credit?   Yes   No

3. Pass/fail   or   graded   (circle one)

4. Total contact hours: _____

5. Hours per session: _____

6. Number of weeks class is held: _____

7. Total number of new students: _____

8. Total students enrolled in class: _____

9. Total number of sections: _____; number of sections you taught: _____

10. Number of students passing class: _____

Retention

1. What percentage of the students in your class was retained to the next term?   _____ %

2. Last year, for the same term, what was the percentage of students retained to the second term? _____ %

   To compute term-to-term retention statistics, use the following formula:

   $$\frac{\text{\# students continuing next term}}{\text{\# students initially enrolled in course}} = \text{term-to-term retention}$$

   For example, 56 students enrolled in your course. From the registrar or other source, you find that 42 of the original 56 are attending classes during the next term.

   $$\frac{42}{56} = .75 \quad \text{or} \quad 75\% \text{ term-to-term retention}$$

   Use this same formula with last year's enrollment figures for the first and second terms in order to compare retention rates from year to year.

We encourage you to maintain retention statistics for each new group of students through the end of their college program.

Copyright © Houghton Mifflin Company. All rights reserved.

The Critical Incident Classroom Questionnaire

Please take about five minutes to respond to each of the following questions about today's class. Don't put your name on the form—your responses are anonymous. When you have finished writing, put the form on the table by the door. At the start of the next class, I will be sharing the responses with the group. Thanks for taking the time to do this. What you write will help me make this class more responsive to your concerns.

1. At what moment today did you feel most engaged with what was happening?

2. At what moment in class did you feel most distanced from what was happening?

3. What actions by the teacher and/or students did you find most affirming and helpful?

4. What actions by the teacher and/or students did you find most puzzling or confusing?

5. What about the class this week surprised you the most? What will you use?

Acknowledgment to Stephen D. Brookfield, *Becoming a Critically Reflective Teacher.*

Copyright © Houghton Mifflin Company. All rights reserved.

College Survival Course Research

In a previous issue of the Student Success newsletter, we presented an excerpt from the *Primer for Research on the Freshman Year Experience* by Dorothy Fidler. We continue to focus on the imperative to examine and thereby improve college survival courses by sharing some of the current research being done.

Corinne Kliegl, tutor coordinator at Des Moines Area Community College (DMACC) in Ankeny, IA, submitted the following freshman seminar data.

The freshman seminar course Orientation to College (CDEV 100) is a one-credit hour, graded, elective course. Its target audience is first-time liberal arts students enrolling for seven credits or more. Currently, we are in the process of making the course required. In order to gather valid data to support the importance of the course, we initiated five pilot classes. A total of 84 students enrolled in the sections offered on three of the five campuses. This course was taught by faculty, counselors, and professional staff. The course purpose is to introduce students to the college's expectations, environment, and resources so that they might become more competent participants in the teaching/learning process.

The following data was based on student evaluation forms, shown below, that were completed after every class period by each student throughout the semester. Evaluation responses range from "strongly agree" to "strongly disagree," and students rated each class based on their understanding of the purpose of the class, student participation in class activities, completion of assignments, and instructor preparation.

94% of the responses were in the "strongly agree" and "agree" category
 4% of the responses were in the "neutral" category
 1% of the responses were in the "disagree" and "strongly disagree" category

The final student evaluation form, completed at the end of the semester, was based on the course competencies.

91% of the responses were in the "strongly agree" and "agree" category
 8% of the responses were in the "neutral" category
 1% of the responses were in the "disagree" and "strongly disagree" category

In addition, data was gathered on the students enrolled in CDEV 100. The preliminary findings were as follows:

62% passed with a C or better
36% earned D, F, or W
76% were first-term students
76% re-enrolled in the spring semester
50% of students with D, F, or W re-enrolled in the spring semester
94% of students with a C or better re-enrolled in the spring semester

Average cumulative GPA of DMACC students—2.54
Average cumulative GPA of students enrolled in CDEV 100 in the fall—1.86
% of students enrolled in CDEV 100 with a cumulative GPA of 2.00 or higher—50%

Student Course Evaluation

1. Did you understand the purpose of the class today?
2. Did you participate in class activities?
3. Did you complete the assignments for this class?
4. Was your instructor prepared for class?
5. Did your instructor include a variety of activities?
6. Did these activities contribute to your understanding of the class material?
7. Did you find the content useful?
8. Would you recommend that this lesson be included in future classes?
9. Are you glad you attended class today?
10. What did you like most about the class?
11. What did you like least about the class?

Copyright © Houghton Mifflin Company. All rights reserved.